I

Question Your Life

**Naikan Self-Reflection
and the
Transformation of Our Stories**

Edited by
Gregg Krech

Published by:
ToDo Institute Books
P.O. Box 50
Monkton, VT 05469
http://www.todoinstitute.org
http://www.thirtythousanddays.org

Interior design: Gerald Sprankel
Cover image: Ookawaphoto
Cover Design: Amanda Coyle

Printed in the United States of America
This edition is printed on acid-free paper.

The Library of Congress catalogs this title as follows:

Krech, Gregg.
Question Your Life: Naikan Self-Reflection and the Transformation of our Stories.
Library of Congress Control Number: 2017947889

ISBN: 978-0-9824273-3-0 (paperback.)
Digital Book ISBN: Pending

Portions of this book originally appeared in different form in the quarterly journal, *Thirty Thousand Days: A Journal for Living on Purpose*

Dedication

To the three women who have shaped me more than anyone else in the past 25 years: My wife, Linda. And my daughters, Chani and Bi. Thank you for being my family.

Comments about
Question Your Life

While we can't change the past, we can change our attitude towards it, and thereby change our future. Building on his previous book, *Naikan: Gratitude, Grace, and the Japanese Art of Self-Reflection*, Krech provides readers with stories and prompts for inner development, gradually leading them through the stages of Naikan reflection. Readers will finish this book with new insights into their life, an enriched gratitude, and a deeper personal understanding of the keys to happiness.

- Chikako Ozawa-de Silva, Ph.D. Associate Professor, Emory University

Question Your Life is perhaps my favorite of Gregg Krech's books, and I've loved all of them. It is at once inspiring, practical, powerful, and so very important. If you want to lead a more honest, humble life with greater integrity, and in the process receive the fruits of joy, gratitude, and a diminishment of regret, read this book. If you want your relationships with others to be more authentic and healthy, answer this book's simple but profound questions. If you want to be a force for good in the world, allow this book's wisdom to set you on the right path. *Question Your Life* is a gift."

- Zoe Weil, Author of The World Becomes What We Teach: Educating a Generation of Solutionaries

When we finally tire of our dusty old stories of how we have been wronged, of who is to blame, or of what we have been denied, we will be ready to take up Gregg's book. *Question Your Life* offers a way to appreciate our life and to help us move beyond the small world of our resentments. As we go beyond our habitual way of understanding our past, we can begin to see the gifts of our life that we may have been blind to. This book opens a process of illumination and transformation: as we realize that we are more than our old stories, we can let go of the weight of our pain and allow space for a deep sense of gratitude to emerge. This is not easy work, but those who are willing and ready to take it up will find *Question Your Life* a trustworthy and valuable guide.

- Ron Hogen Green, Sensei — Zen Center of New York City

Question Your Life is a blessing. A balm to the soul for allowing us not only to see with new eyes and be inspired, but more importantly it offers us a simple way to gently change our course. Through a variety of voices, we "hear" and are moved to consider a doable and kind way to reduce suffering in the world – our own and others.

- Trudy Boyle, Chairperson, North American Naikan Council

Table of Contents

Be patient toward all that is unsolved in your heart
and to try to love the questions themselves
like locked rooms and like books that are written
in a very foreign tongue.
Do not now seek the answers,
which cannot be given you
because you would not be able to live them.
And the point is, to live everything.
Live the questions now.

~ Rainer Maria Rilke

Introduction

S uppose you arrive at a party. The host greets you at the door and says there is someone he'd like you to meet. You follow him into the next room and the person he introduces you to is . . . you! That's right, he introduces you to yourself. What would your experience be? You know this person better than anyone, don't you? After all, you have the same history, the same parents, you're the same height and weight.

But something about this person seems different in a strange sort of way. She doesn't look exactly like you. She has some mannerisms and ways of speaking that you don't have – at least you don't think you have them. As you talk, you discover things about the person that you didn't know – or perhaps you just forgot. This person isn't an exact copy – she's not quite the person you thought she would be. You find yourself both curious and confused. Uneasy, yet somehow relieved. How fascinating! You've actually encountered yourself! Extraordinary!

A young man approaches you from the right. He offers to refill your glass with more wine. You hesitate, but then consent to just a bit more. You watch as he pours the wine carefully into your glass and stop him politely when he reaches the half-way point.

When you turn your head, the person you met – you – is no longer there. She's vanished.

How well do you know yourself? If you're like most people, you think you know yourself pretty well. But take a moment and examine yourself. Let's start with your physical body. Examine your body as thoroughly as possible. You'll quickly realize there are large areas of your body you can't see. You can't see your back. You can't see much of your butt. You can't see the back, or front, of your neck. And you can't see your head at all (well, maybe a bit of your nose). Your head is the part of you that is most exposed, because there are no clothes covering it up. It's the part of your body that houses your brain and displays all your facial expressions. It is where your eyes reside, the part of you that sees the faces and heads of those around you. Yet you have no idea what your head looks like, do you?

Well, of course you do, because you've looked in a mirror. A mirror gives you a way to see yourself. You probably use one regularly – perhaps even several times each day. But a mirror, though useful, has significant limitations. You're only able to see your physical appearance and that's a very superficial representation of a person. It doesn't reveal the inner landscape of a human being. It doesn't reveal whether the person is healthy or ill. It doesn't reveal one's intelligence. It doesn't reveal the degree to which a person may be selfish or generous. It doesn't reveal thoughts, dreams and fantasies. And it doesn't reveal the essence, the true nature, of who that person really is.

For us to truly understand ourselves, we have to use a tool that allows us to go beyond the capabilities of a mirror. Way beyond.

The Ghost of Christmas Past

To be perfectly honest, you're a bit freaked out after meeting yourself. You suspect that someone slipped some kind of strange drug in your drink. Or maybe in the other person's drink – the person that is also you. Anyway, you don't really buy this idea of "knowing yourself" and "self-awareness." Too much like psychotherapy or meditation or something from the '60s. No thanks. You have things to do and places to go. No need for introspection. No point in gazing at one's navel. People should just set goals, work hard, and move forward. Let's just get on with it.

So you gracefully move through the crowd into the next room where people are gathered around a big screen TV watching a movie. It's the Charles Dicken's classic, *The Christmas Carol* (Did I mention it's a Christmas party?). There are many versions, but this happens to be the Jim Carrey version – not your favorite but you appreciate the special effects. This is the part where Ebenezer Scrooge is guided by the ghost of Christmas past to see some of his own past. Some of it is sad. Some of it is sweet. He has regrets. But the past can't be changed − only observed. Only remembered. And sometimes . . . there is something to be learned.

As the movie unfolds, you begin to think about your own past. There were so many decisions: where you went to school, accepting your first real job, breaking up with that girl or guy, moving to a different city. Each of those decisions was a stepping stone that led to where you are right now. Had you made a different decision, even a small one, your life could be completely different.

Who Are You?

As you stand there sipping a glass of Chardonnay, your host wanders over and starts asking you questions.

"What time did you arrive at the party?"

"About 9 p.m.," you say.

"Are you sure?" he inquires.

"I'm fairly sure," you respond. "Maybe a few minutes after 9."

"Have you eaten any of the snacks since you arrived?" asks your host.

"Yes," you respond. "I had some tortilla chips and a few baby carrots with dip."

"Are you sure?" says the host.

"Yes," you say, feeling slightly uncomfortable. "What is the purpose of your questions?"

"Just curious," says the host. He continues.

"Where do you live?" he asks.

"I live at 785 Bridgewater Street."

"Are you sure?" he asks.

"Absolutely. I've lived there for two years."

"And where did you live as a child?"

You pause to think. You grew up in Glenview, Illinois. What was the address? Aha!

You remember.

"I lived at 7209 Chandler Street in Glenview, Illinois. That was my first home. I grew up there as a child."

"Are you sure?" he asks. "Are you sure you didn't live somewhere prior to that?"

"No, I grew up there. It's the only place I lived until I left for college,"

you state confidently. But wait . . . that's not true. You were born in a hospital on the north side of Chicago and you lived in the city until your parents moved to that house in Glenview when you were two years old. You don't remember that. But your parents showed you pictures of yourself and the apartment. So actually, that apartment was the first place you ever lived. You explain to your host that you were mistaken. That you actually lived in an apartment until you were two.

"Very good," says the host. "I just have one more question. I'm curious. 'Who are you?' he asks," looking directly into your eyes.

You chuckle, "That's silly. Well, I'm me, of course." "Me," you say. "This person standing right in front of you."

"Do you see those baby carrots over there?" he says. "Are those carrots you?"

"Of course not," you say. "Those are carrots. I am me." You laugh.

"You have a carrot in your right hand at this moment. Is that carrot you?" he says.

"No," you state confidently, starting to think about how long you're willing to continue playing this inane game.

"How about the carrots you ate?" he asks. "Are those you?"

Hmmm. You think for a moment. "Well, yes," you say. "They're in my stomach, so I would say they are me."

"So the carrot in your hand isn't you, but the carrot in your stomach is. Is that right?"

"Well yes," you say. "I would say that's a reasonable way to look at it."

Your host picks up a book. The title of the book is *Man's Search for Meaning* by Viktor Frankl. You recognize it. You read it many years ago.

"Is this book you?" he asks.

"Of course not," you say. "I haven't eaten it yet," you reply in an attempt to be witty.

"Have you read it?"

"Yes, many years ago."

"Do you remember anything from the book?"

You think. "Yes, as a matter of fact I do. I remember the analogy that suffering is like a gas and it will expand to fill the receptacle regardless of its size, whether the suffering is great or little. So Frankl suggests that human suffering is always relative." Your posture straightens and you feel a tinge of pride in your memory.

"So is the idea you?" asks your host.

"Well, the idea isn't mine. It comes from Viktor Frankl."

"Then how did you know it?"

"I told you, I read the book years ago."

"But where was the idea just now, just before you mentioned it to me?"

"Well, it was in my head. Or rather, in my mind."

"So is your mind you?"

This is getting a bit too "deep" for you. You came here to enjoy yourself not to get grilled with stupid questions that have no purpose. But before you can respond, your host says, "You know, I don't think I know who you are. But I'm sure you don't know who you are. If you'll excuse me, I have something I need to attend to."

The Questioning Spirit

The renowned Indian pandita, Aryadeva, was the principle disciple of the great Buddhist teacher, Nagarjuna. Aryadeva once said, *"to merely question that things might not be as they seem can shake the very foundation of habitual clinging."*

Pythagoras questioned whether the earth was flat. Aristotle questioned whether the earth was flat. Magellan proved the earth was round by sailing around the entire world. This questioning spirit changed the way we understand the shape of the world we live in.

If you're willing to question your life, it may change the way you understand your own world . . . your own life.

Let's start with a simple question: *What made it possible for you to be here?* "Here" is where you are at this very moment in time and space. What made it possible? Can you bookmark this page and pause for 3–4 minutes to reflect on this question? When you hold this question in your mind/heart, what comes up for you?

Pause.

Note: This Is the Part Where You Are Reflecting

Let me share what comes up for me. At this moment I am sitting in the living room of the ToDo Institute in Vermont – the retreat center where I teach, write and conduct programs.

The first thing that surfaces in my own mind are my parents. Without them, I wouldn't be here. I'm also aware of Susan King, who sold the organization this wonderful 12 acre property. Some of the people who made this place a reality, through their support include Sue Cole, Barbara Sarah, Ron Hogen Green, John Waters, David Reynolds, and Bob Rauseo. They helped finance the initial purchase of the property. My good friend Ron Heatley helped us on moving day. My wife was willing to move to Vermont and support my work as I created a nonprofit organization and put together the elements of a functioning organization 25 years ago. Then there are my teachers that encouraged me and helped me journey down my own path of personal and spiritual self-reflection: Rev. Kenryu Tsuji, Rev. Shue Usami, Ven. Thich Nhat Hanh, Professor Akira Ishii, Mrs. Yoshimoto Ishin, and Nagashima sensei. My friend, Perri Ardman, connected me with Peter Goodman at Stone Bridge Press, who published my first book on Naikan.

I'll stop there for now.

A few years ago, I read the book, A Short History of Nearly Everything, in which author Bill Bryson added a somewhat different perspective to the question, "What made it possible to be here?"

"For you to be here now, trillions of drifting atoms had somehow to assemble in an intricate and intriguingly obliging manner to create you. It's an arrangement so specialized and particular that it has never been tried before and will exist only this once. For the next many years (we hope) these tiny particles will uncomplainingly engage in all the billions of deft, cooperative efforts necessary to keep you intact and let you experience the supremely agreeable, but generally underappreciated state known as existence."

He goes on to say,

"The only thing that's special about the atoms that make you is that they make you. That is, of course, the miracle of life."

Beyond the miracle of my atomic engineering is my ancestry. I mentioned my parents, but without my grandparents they wouldn't have been here to bring me to life. I can say this about each previous generation. How far back shall I go? Well, I am here because each of my genetic ancestors provided what was necessary to bring the next generation of ancestors into existence. For me to be here, now, each of them, without a single exception, had to stay alive, find a partner and procreate. Amazing!

It's rare that we really appreciate the fact that we are alive. Being alive doesn't seem so delightful when we're in pain, when we're grieving, when we're angry and when we're deeply disappointed. At times like this, we don't really experience life as a blessing.

Additionally, most things we appreciate can be considered in the context of their absence. We have food, but we know what it's like to be hungry. We have money, but we know what it's like to be broke. We have companionship, but we know what it's like to be alone. The same is probably true of electricity, heat, music, transportation, and perhaps even mobility (walking). We appreciate the gifts of life, because we have experienced life, at least temporarily, without those gifts.

But what about life itself? Unless you have actually been dead and resuscitated, you don't really know what it's like not to be alive. We have no experience of "not-life" to compare to being alive. When we wake up on a sunny Sunday morning and look at a blue sky we know what it's like when the sky is cloudy or when it's dark. But we don't know what it's like to not be there to see the sky. We don't know what it's like to not exist. We don't often appreciate life because the alternative is beyond our comprehension.

7

Your Research Project

You're unlikely to meet yourself at a party – solitude is more conducive to this kind of experience. You have to disengage with the world around you – with people, with gadgets, with music, even with loved ones. You have to find a place and time where you can quietly work on your research project. The object of your research is incredibly important to you.

Your research project is your life.

The results of your research will inform your choices and your conduct from this point forward until you die. What you learn from this research project – your analysis and conclusions – will have an impact on your relationship with your friends, parents, partner, children and colleagues. It can affect your family, your community and even the world. Don't take it lightly.

What do you need for this project?

Solitude
Time
Courage and Sincerity
Questions
A Method of Collecting Data

This is not a collaborative project. You are the sole researcher. You have funding. You're on a tight time frame because you don't know when time will run out. If you spent a few minutes reflecting on the question, "What made it possible for you to be here?" you've already started your research.

Keep up the good work.

Fortune Cookies

Back at the party you decide to leave the room where The Christmas Carol is being shown. Scrooge is about to go on his tour with the Ghost of Christmas Future.

8

He's going to get a glimpse of his future. You wonder what it would be like to get a glimpse of your own future. Would it be interesting to know what was going to happen for the rest of the year? Or the next year? But what if there was something tragic, like an accident or a terminal illness? Would you really want to know that if there was no way to avoid it?

You wander back to a buffet that is stocked with snacks. On the table is a silver platter with baby carrots and artichoke dip. Next to it is a large blue ceramic bowl with tortilla chips accompanied by a smaller bowl of salsa. You pause. Which one should you eat? Then you notice something curious – sitting on top of the baby carrots is a single fortune cookie, just like the ones you might find in a Chinese restaurant. There's also a fortune cookie on top of the bowl of tortilla chips. That's strange, you think. I don't remember seeing any fortune cookies here before.

You reach for the fortune cookie on top of the chips. You open it and pull out the small white paper buried in the fold of the cookie and pull it taut. It says,

"You create the future by what you do now."

Interesting, you think.

You then reach for the other fortune cookie, the one sitting atop the baby carrots. You break the cookie and open the small paper inside. This one says,

"You create the past by what you do now."

You pause and read it a second time. You're a bit baffled by this one. What does that mean, "you create the past by what you do now."

You decide to call it a night. To head home. You leave the broken cookies, uneaten, on the buffet table. You create the past by what you do now.

A Traveling Storyteller

If you go to an airport you'll notice that nearly everyone is carrying some type of suitcase or bag. Inside are belongings they've chosen to take on their trip. The contents often include objects like a toothbrush, a wallet, a hairbrush, underwear, books, a cell phone, etc. Most people give some thought to what they pack. They think about where they're going and ask themselves, "What will I need on my journey?"

"I'm going to my in-laws for the holidays, what will I need?"

"I'm going camping for the weekend, what will I need?"

"I'm going to travel around Ireland for three weeks, what will I need?"

When we travel, we have limited space in our bags. We try to take only what's important and leave the rest behind.

We would be wise to treat our stories the same way. We carry around our stories in our mind and heart (the Japanese have a single word for mind/heart – kokoro). Some of these stories don't serve us very well.

Do you have a story, or several, that you've been carrying with you? Were you neglected as a child? Were you abandoned? Was your father evil? Was your life ruined by your first husband or wife? Is it that you spent so much time taking care of everyone else that your own needs were ignored? Are you a victim? My story was family violence. What is your story?

We've often solidified these stories based on our emotions and a limited selection of facts. But we've left out many facts and experiences that don't support our story. We take these stories with us on our journey and treat them as solid truths.

"To merely question that things might not be as they seem can shake the very foundation of habitual clinging."

Many of these stories aren't worth the space they're occupying in our minds. They serve no useful purpose. They leave us feeling resentful, angry and unloved. They contribute to a view of ourselves as victims and cost us our faith. Yet we travel with them constantly. Why? First, because we don't recognize them for what they are – believed stories. Second, because we don't know how to get rid of them. It's like an odor coming from your suitcase, but you don't know where the odor is coming from. And you can't get rid of it.

The experiences described in this book are from people who discovered how to repack their suitcase. They used self-reflection – a method called Naikan, developed in Japan – to repack their bags and change the way they journey through life. The essays that follow provide practical guidance and spiritual inspiration. They offer you a way to question your life.

This questioning spirit is the starting point for self-reflection.

Are you willing to question your story? It's not easy. For some of us, that story is a big part of our identity. We do not easily give it up. If we give up our story, who are we? If you were no longer a victim, who would you be?

The Questions

Earlier in the introduction, I offered you a question: What made it possible for you to be here? This is a wonderful question to launch you on your research project. But the best method I've discovered for questioning your life (collecting your research data) is a method from Japan called Naikan. When I wrote my first book on Naikan, in 2002, I researched actual methodologies for self-reflection. The most popular is the Twelve-step Program used by Alcoholics Anonymous – particularly the fourth step. There are other methods, including The Examen developed by St. Ignatius of Loyola and a personal system of self-reflection used by Benjamin Franklin. But, for the most part, there is a great deal of encouragement in spiritual traditions to reflect on oneself, yet a great absence of structured methodologies for how to do so.

The method I have used personally and professionally for the past thirty years is called Naikan (pronounced the way Americans pronounce the camera Nikon). It was originally developed by a Japanese man named Ishin Yoshimoto (1916 – 1988) in the late 1930's. He had personally engaged in a traditional practice of self-reflection called mishirabe. Mishirabe was an intense spiritual practice associated with the Pure Land sect of Buddhism in Japan. Subsequently, Yoshimoto developed Naikan as a secular

11

method of self-reflection that would be accessible to anyone interested in a process of self-examination.

Naikan is primarily built on a foundation of three questions – simple questions, yet potentially revealing. Suppose you're going to reflect on your relationship with your partner, or perhaps a close friend. In most cases, we use a relationship as a basis for reflection. That relationship is our mirror.

The first two questions are:

1. What have I received from _____?
2. What have I given to _____?

Quite simple, really. You're just looking at the give and take in the relationship. The third question is more challenging.

In my relationships with parents, children, colleagues, teachers, friends, and partners, I'm very familiar with what it is like for me to have to deal with the other person. I know what the other person does that bothers me, agitates me and irritates me. And I know what they don't do that causes me distress, as well. But I'm not nearly as familiar with what it is like for the other person.

What is it like for Linda to be married to me?
What is it like for Abbie to have me as a father?
What is it like for Blaze to have me as a friend?
What is it like for Robert to work with me during a retreat?

The third question offers an opportunity to put yourself in the other person's shoes. What is the experience of the other person? More specifically, what is their experience dealing with you? The third question is:

3. What troubles and difficulties have I caused _____?

By using a relationship as the subject of my reflection, I have a framework for questioning my life.

As you can see, the questions are straight-forward. Even young children can understand them. Yet they can have a profound impact on how you understand yourself, your relationships and your life.

12

How can such a simple process have a profound effect on your experience of life and your relationship with others? The essays in this book provide real examples of people who had a turn of the mind as a result of quiet self-reflection. A woman who hated her mother, a man estranged from his father, a woman with cancer, a pregnant woman who is hit by a train. A couple struggling with their marriage and even a rabbi who neglected his shoes.

But the best way to test out this process is to try it yourself. At the end of this book I've offered some specific instructions on how to reflect on yourself at home. Or perhaps someday you'll choose to go on retreat and spend 100 hours examining your life. What would you discover if you did that?

The Book of Your Life

Imagine that everything you've ever done, from the moment of your birth, was recorded in a book. This is the book of your life. How much of the book has been written? Thirty percent? Fifty percent? Eighty-five percent? You don't really know. Today could be the last page.

Though the pages are numbered
I can't see where they lead
For the end is a mystery no-one can read
in the book of my life
- Sting

If you could read the entire book right now, there might be some things you would want to change. Perhaps there were times when you were mean or selfish. Perhaps there were circumstances where you lied or deceived others. Perhaps there were occasions where you failed to act with integrity. But you can't change the book. What is written is written. Many of the stories you have in your suitcase do not reflect what's in the book. Those stories are edited. They're often edited to make us look good

– to justify our own behavior. But the rest of the book is not yet written. There are blank pages waiting for you. What will they say in a year? In five years? How will the book end?

Wondering

A few days later you walk into a coffee shop and sitting in a booth in the corner is the host of the recent party you attended. You approach the booth.

"Hi, remember me. Are you alone? I'm wondering if I can join you for a moment and ask you a question."

"I'm not alone," he says. "Nobody's alone. But you're welcome to join me."

"The other night, at the party, I met someone who appeared to be me. For a few moments, I thought I actually encountered myself. Then she disappeared. I'm wondering whether it was just a dream or perhaps I just imagined the whole thing."

"You didn't imagine it," he says. "You had a brief glimpse of yourself. It was just long enough for you to realize that you're not who you think you are. Now you're curious, which is good. But to discover something important, you have to investigate. Most people don't take the time for this kind of investigation. They're too busy. There are places to go, errands to run, emails to check, things to buy and people to meet. Most people don't take time to investigate their life and who they are. St. Augustine once said,

> *"People travel to wonder*
> *at the height of the mountains,*
> *at the huge waves of the seas,*
> *at the long course of the rivers,*
> *at the vast compass of the ocean,*
> *at the circular motion of the stars,*
> *and yet they pass by themselves*
> *without wondering."*

"The other day you passed by yourself and now you're wondering. So now what will you do?"

"What is it I should do?" you ask.

"You just did it. You asked a question. But you shouldn't be asking me. I have no answers for you."

"Well, who should I ask then?"

He just smiles, but says nothing.

"I'm really new to this. I don't know where to begin."

"Just begin with your curiosity. Investigate. Examine the stories you have come to believe about how you have lived. Question yourself. Question who you are. Question your life."

Having Tea
with People from
Our Past

Introduction
by Gregg Krech

For many of us, childhood is a turbulent time. It may be marked by conflict, marital discord, serious illness, sibling rivalry, financial anxiety, violence, social struggle, addiction and even death. While we struggle to discover who we are and what we wish to become, our parents struggle to juggle the demands of parenting, while trying to maintain a household, a job, and, perhaps, a healthy partnership. As a parent, we receive training for none of this. We are incompetent from the beginning. As a child, we hold our parents accountable for their failures. In many cases the stories we weave come from threads of disappointment and resentment. We weren't loved. Or we weren't loved enough. Or we were loved imperfectly. Or whatever love we received was corrupted by the myriad ways in which we were hurt or neglected.

Wearing a garment of disappointment, resentment and anger is a great burden. It continuously weighs us down as we try to move forward in our lives. The toxicity of this story-garment leaches into our relationships with our own partners. It affects our fundamental view of life. It buries us in a complaint-based lifestyle in which our attention is consistently drawn to what is going wrong and how the world fails to meet our expectations. We blame others, particularly our parents, for why our lives are messed up.

When I left for college at the age of 18, I couldn't wait to get out of my parent's home. My story was one of *family violence*. While some of this violence was directed toward me, much of it took place between my parents. Police were called on multiple occasions. Sometimes by me. As I grew up, I discovered strategies of either leaving the house or going into the basement and turning up the volume on the stereo. I developed a deep sense of hostility toward my parents as a teenager. I blamed one, then the other, then both, for my unhappy childhood.

Though I escaped from my childhood home, I didn't escape from the story I had created. It came with me to college and stayed with me as my life unfolded. It continued to have a direct influence on my relationship with family members and, more subtly, to permeate my attitude towards life overall. I was self-centered, critical, ungrateful and willful. Beyond that, I had no basis for faith or trust in anything beyond my own efforts.

At the age of 33, as a result of an interest in Eastern Philosophy and Buddhism, I found myself in a Naikan center in Japan. Surrounded by rice fields, my only mission was to spend about 200 hours, for two weeks, reflecting on my life. That reflection began with my mother. Using the structure of Naikan's three questions (see the Introduction, page 18) I traced the give and take between my mother and me from as far back as I could remember. I spent the entire first day – 15 hours – considering nothing but what I had received from her, what I had given to her, and how I had caused her trouble. This was both a practical and spiritual reconciliation of my relationship with her. I was aware of my stiff resistance to this process, even as I became aware of the crack which was forming in my granite-like resentment toward her.

As I proceeded through this reflection on her, in three year increments, I received almost no guidance. I worked with the structure that was given to me – the questions, the three-year period of reflection, and the sharing of what I remembered with a staff member or "guide" who would meet with me every two hours. But there was no discussion, no analysis, no judgment and no praise or criticism of my efforts. My support for this process took the form of heartfelt listening, food and a place to sleep. The contemplation I was doing – emotionally, psychologically and spiritually – I was doing on my own. Or at least that is how I understood it at the time.

I went through the second day of my retreat examining my relationship with my father. As I recalled the details of my childhood and my early adult years, details were emerging that began to challenge my story. I was given piano lessons, swimming lessons, medical appointments, birthday parties, rides to school, Christmas gifts, help with car repairs, even bologna sandwiches and Twinkies wrapped securely in a brown paper bag that was prepared for my lunch at elementary school.

Nothing in my reflections led me to believe that my family violence story didn't happen. Nothing made me question the validity of those experiences and memories. It's just that the story was filling out. There were pages and pages of support, care and gifts that were missing from my original story. And beyond that, there were pages of my own transgressions, including lying, deceit and selfishness that were now populating the book of my life. I was not an innocent victim – certainly not during my teenage years.

The time I spent reflecting on my parents during this retreat in Japan, and in subsequent retreats, transformed my relationship with them. My relationship with my father blossomed into a closeness that had us eventually traveling together to places like England, Alaska, New Orleans, Montreal, Vancouver, Florida and elsewhere. He visited me regularly when I lived in Virginia and drove the U-haul truck from Virginia to Vermont where my wife and I were married. He died in my arms in a Chicago hospice as I stroked his forehead. The conflict and hostility that occurred between us during my youth were now relegated to the distant past and I found both compassion and appreciation for him as I realized what a struggle it was for him to cope with his own life during my childhood years.

He wasn't an ideal father. He was a good father that was deeply devoted to me even when I couldn't see it.

The transformation of my relationship with my mother was less grand. We didn't travel together or become best friends. But I discovered a growing sense of acceptance of her, and patience with her as I remembered that she changed thousands of my dirty diapers – a memory that I could resurrect strategically during phone conversations where I found her words agitating and provocative. I came to the conclusion that my mother did an exceptional job of being who she was, even though it wasn't always who I wanted her to be. When I ceased trying to change her and, instead, focused on just being her son, we were able to settle into a less contentious connection that carried us through to the end of her life.

I credit Naikan reflection for opening both my eyes and my heart to my parents' love, and for moving me to a place of greater acceptance that was, in part, built upon the recognition of my own limitations and faults. My own weaknesses as a parent are prominent, though they don't necessarily match those of my mother and father. My father's devotion to me is an ideal that I strive for in my devotion to my daughters. And, to be honest, both my children are much easier to parent than I was.

Not everyone will have the opportunity to reflect on their parents while their parents are alive. But when we reflect on them we have an opportunity to rewrite our stories so they more accurately represent the original draft – the draft that took place in reality, rather than our minds. We can create a story more grounded in fact and less tainted by the emotional coloring of our confusion, anxiety, resentment and anger as we unfolded into adulthood.

There is nothing in Naikan reflection that condones violence or abuse by a parent towards a child. Spiritual and psychological contemplation is not designed to deny our suffering, for we all have suffered. In fact, it's the recognition that we all have suffered that allows us to be released from the illusion that somehow our suffering is special – somehow it is worse than the suffering of others. When we see people at work or social gatherings, we see people making their best effort to function despite the suffering that occupies their life in the present and past. We may assume that these people "have their act together." But in reality, in the privacy of their bedrooms, in the confidential corners of their relationships, and in the recesses of a mind which harbors their fears, anxieties and regrets about life, they suffer as well.

One of the gifts of Naikan, of quiet contemplation, is that it allows us to see beyond our suffering into how we were cared for and loved. And sometimes, it allows us to see suffering itself as having been the messenger of grace. For many of us, this discovery can only be made in retrospect. For some of us, self-reflection will paint the way we understand the present, and open doors to a future that would otherwise have remained bolted shut.

Puffed up by our self-will, we look out at the world through the distorting medium of our likes and dislikes, hopes and fears, and opinions and judgments. We want everyone to behave as we think they should – the right way. When, naturally enough, they not only behave their own way, but expect us to do as they do, we get agitated. And what we see through this agitation makes up our everyday reality.

- Eknath Easwaran

A Scroll Was Found Between Two Hearts

by Romola Georgia

My mother was 96 years old when she died last month. This tiny woman, child of immigrants from the Ukraine, lived through World Wars I and II, the Great Depression, and countless economic and political upheavals. Her childhood was cruelly marked by a misguided radiation treatment that destroyed her health and physical well-being. She never expected to live past age 50 (when both her parents died). Had she died 46 years ago, I would be writing a very different story.

I grew up during the thrill of psychology's early promise, and we were a very modern family. When I seemed moody or sullen or jealous of my brother, help was available in the form of therapy. I began play therapy at a very young age and wandered through a succession of experts promising to relieve me – and my family – of myriad uncomfortable feelings. As I matured, I hardened into the certainty that my mother was the true cause of my psychological problems. She was the villain in our family – the root of all our unhappiness and misery.

It was quite easy to build a case for the many ways my mother caused me difficulties. Her illness kept her in bed a fair amount of the time and I grew to resent the dark bedroom and silent house. She didn't cook much and got flustered and uncertain when she tried. My thoughts about her traveled well-worn paths: *She is clearly negligent in her motherly duties. No special projects or outings at our house. Why did I have to miss out on the good stuff that normal families did? Why did I get stuck with this awful psychosomatic mother instead of the superior healthy models that most of my friends had?*

I detected in my mother toxic levels of inferiority and self-doubt and judged her conversations with friends and relatives as painful games of name-dropping and one-upmanship. By the time I was an adult participating in a 12-step program, I concluded that my mother's pain, fear, suffering, self-doubt, and insecurity had actually migrated from her body to mine in utero while I was defenseless and unprotected. Being the child of such a woman had clearly ruined my life.

25

Even as an adult, I rarely took pains to disguise my contempt and resentment toward my mother. I decided that the vast gaps in my memories of childhood were due to the abuse and neglect I must have experienced. At times I was barely civil. I can remember angling my chair so as not to have to look at her while dining together; just seeing my mother's face stimulated paroxysms of judgment and self-pity.

I only began to see our relationship and our family dynamic differently when I learned about Naikan, a structured form of self-reflection that invited me to explore this relationship using the following three questions:

What have I received from my mother?
What have I given to my mother?
What troubles and difficulties have I caused my mother?

I first encountered Naikan in a continuing studies class at Stanford University and quickly grasped what a practical and insightful tool it was for improving relationships. I had the opportunity to spend about an hour reflecting on my mother during a weekend retreat my husband and I attended. But it was only several years later, after both my own daughters had attended weeklong Naikan retreats at the ToDo Institute, that I finally committed to making my own seven-day retreat. The first day of the Naikan retreat is devoted to one's mother, the core relationship for most folks. I was terribly worried about the scant recollection I had of my early years. Most of my memories seemed to be manufactured from snapshots straight out of my childhood photo album.

But, bit by bit, I remembered. The reflection required that I consider our relationship from her perspective: *What was it like for my mother to have me as a daughter?* I slowly and very imperfectly began shifting away from my habitual focus on myself – **my** needs, **my** desires, **my** perceptions, **my** ideas... The resolute focus and the long hours spent reflecting on my mother through each phase of my own 60-plus years of life gradually sculpted important changes in my understanding. I was coming to see a truer picture of our reality, one that helped me begin to let go of the story of my childhood and my family that had dominated my life.

I noted that despite my mother's illness, I had been fed and clothed and housed throughout the years of my helpless babyhood. *How many diapers had she changed?* I wondered. *Which vegetables and fruits had she pureed and fed me a spoonful at a time?* I very clearly remembered all the lessons and enrichment I received: tap dance, ballet, Girl Scouts, and summer camps as a kid. Then as a teen: cello lessons, orchestra, chamber music, and music camp. For the first time, I thought about the arduous scheduling and transportation that enabled me to attend rehearsals, recitals and concerts that were the foundation of my lifelong joy and participation in music.

Not only did my mom send me to an excellent college, but she also supported me when I breezed off to Mexico the summer of my first year, and even when I dropped out of school and moved to California after my second year. What worries and anxieties did she endure? As a young adult, much of my travel, adventure, and shopping were courtesy of my mother. And in later years, she made it possible for me to purchase a home and was kind and generous to my own children.

When I came to reflect on the second question, "What have I given to my mother?" I found myself facing a huge blank wall. Excruciating focus yielded little in the way of love, kindness, or appreciation I had ever offered to her. Material gifts were likewise, pretty skimpy. In Girl Scouts, I made my mother a pair of trivets out of little stone blocks. I also brought her a painted bowl from Mexico made from a gourd. I found both these gifts while cleaning out her house after she died. They were precious evidence of the meager repayment I made in return for her lifetime of generosity and caring.

What troubles and difficulties did I cause my mother? This third question forced me to take a hard look at reality. My glib, well-practiced story about my deprived childhood had already taken a beating. I also had to face the inconsistency between my view of myself as a good and loving person and the indifference and habitual cruelty I had dealt out to my own mother. My image of the "ideal mother" had blinded me to the mothering I had, in fact, received. Her support was there all along, but it didn't really register as long as I was preoccupied with my mother's deficits and my own misery. Now a mother myself, I could very easily imagine the pain of being on the receiving end of judgment and disdain from one's own daughter.

I regret that it took me so long to bring the reality of my upbringing into focus and to understand the preciousness of my mother's love. Her long life became an unexpected gift – allowing me to make amends and heal some of the hurt. In the last few years, I was finally able to say thank you for her love and caring. I composed a scroll, listing more than 100 of my mother's gifts to me – as many as I could recall. I rolled it, tied it with a ribbon, and sent it to her in a tiny box. I apologized for my unkindness. The air cleared, the tension dissipated, and my mother and I began to feel complete together.

My mother spent the last few months of her life in hospice care. We got to hold hands, snuggle together, look at old photos, and talk about the past with an intimacy and closeness that would have been unimaginable several years earlier. In looking back, the investment of time and energy made during my Naikan retreat was a sacred way of honoring the loving-kindness of my mother's life. The Naikan reflection helped to heal and transform our relationship, characterized for so long by resentment and tension. I wonder now if, when I am dying, my daughters and I will also be brought together through the bond that flows from our own reflections on each other.

While cleaning out my mother's house, I found the little scroll I had made in the drawer next to her bed. It reminds me how grateful I am for my mother, for the possibility of becoming conscious in my relationships, and for the very gift of life itself.

> *"How much of our distress is rooted in the stories we weave around our experiences? Dropping our story line is critical to being aware of what is actually happening in the present moment. We need to see the story line for what it is and stop rehashing it over and over with our believed thoughts, since all they do is sustain and solidify our painful experiences."*
>
> *Ezra Bayda, Zen Teacher, San Diego Zen Center*

Many Mothers

by Gregg Krech

When Jennifer was a freshman in high school, she slipped in the mud on the far side of the softball field during lunchtime. Jennifer's mom, knowing her daughter was auditioning for the school play that afternoon, abruptly stopped what she was doing and drove to Jennifer's school with a fresh change of clothing.

Jennifer is participating in a Naikan retreat where she is reflecting on her entire life. She just spent two hours reflecting on what she received from her mother during her first three years of high school. She has a long list which includes her mom driving her to piano lessons, making her breakfast almost every morning (that's 1,000+ breakfasts), arranging for her to attend a music camp during summer break, and throwing her a special "sweet sixteen" birthday party. She is also considering the question of what she gave to her mother during those same years, but is having trouble remembering very much and her list is quite brief.

The final question involves reflecting on the troubles and difficulties she caused her mom during that time. She caused a car accident while driving resulting in about $1,800 dollars of damage to the family car. She got in a fight with her sister that ended with her sister going to the emergency room for stitches in her lip (it was an accident, of course). She borrowed her mom's favorite blouse and got blueberry stains on it which never came out. There was a lot more.

Jennifer is 48 years old and it's the first day of her retreat. She'll continue to reflect on her life in relationship to her mother up until the present day. During that time she'll calculate how many loads of laundry her mom did for her and how many dirty dishes her mom washed. At the end of her reflection on her mother, she'll have a clearer sense of the give and take in their relationship. She'll also have a clearer understanding of what it was like to be Jennifer's mother all those years. She already has a good idea of all the things her mother did that agitated, bothered and disappointed her and she's had an easy time holding on to her mother's faults and shortcomings. Her reflections fill in the bigger picture. Now, with time to consciously reflect on her relationship over the years, she recalls all the occasions when she was cared for and loved.

Jennifer's mother is still alive. That means she'll have an opportunity, if she chooses, to express her gratitude in a heartfelt way which is grounded in the awareness of how she was loved. She doesn't have to wait for Mother's Day or her mom's birthday. For others, however, their mothers are no longer alive. They may cultivate a sincere sense of gratitude for their mom's love, but they won't be able to share that gratitude with her. Their thanks can only be expressed in their hearts and in their memories of her.

Perhaps your own mother died when you were young. Or perhaps she actually abandoned you when you were a child so you were raised by an aunt. Or maybe she abandoned you at birth and you were placed in an orphanage. How do you develop a sense of gratitude for a mother who, to be honest, simply wasn't there for you much of your life?

It's pretty difficult to do as long as we see our mother as a single human being. Even if she was around for many years, she probably was imperfect and made mistakes. So I'd like to offer you a different vision of your mother. A vision in which your mother is not an individual human being, but a constellation of many human beings – a force of care, support and loving-kindness which has mothered you since before you were born.

Even if your mother didn't always change your diapers, someone changed them. Even if your mother didn't always make your dinner, someone made you dinner (it may have been the people who put the food in the Swanson frozen dinners you ate when you came home late from school). Someone took care of you when you were sick. Someone tied your shoes before you learned to do it, and then, someone taught you how to tie your shoes yourself. Someone taught you to read and drove you everywhere before you could drive, and someone provided you with shoes and washed your dirty laundry. In some cases, perhaps in many cases, this was your birth mother. In other cases, much of this was done by your adoptive mother. Or perhaps the aunt you lived with when you were a teenager. Or sometimes your grandmother. Or your dad, older brother or uncle.

I'm suggesting a vision of your mother as a team of many people – each one playing a major or minor role in helping you become who you are. So let's include the authors of books that touched your spirit, and the babysitter, and the neighbor who let you play with her puppy. And let's not forget the school nurse who gave you a Band-Aid when you cut your leg at recess and your best friend's mom who used to let you stay for dinner on Fridays after school. If you reflect deeply on your life, you'll find a rather large team of people, some of whom you never met, that offered you mothering throughout your childhood and into your adult years. These people cared for you, supported you, taught you, mended you, transported you, fed you and, in their own way, loved you.

How could we expect one woman, one human being, to handle this huge job? That would be impossible. You probably had one person, a team captain, who took the lead during your childhood. Maybe you had different team leaders at different points in your life. But they were all part of the same team. To really understand how you were loved, and to really have a sense of gratitude in response, you have to see this as a team effort.

This isn't meant to discount the care and extraordinary efforts of the person you refer to as your mother. She may have led that team for many years, and, if so, she deserves a great deal of thanks. She was on the front lines much of the time. If you see that she did a wonderful job, then certainly let her know you realize the depth of her love and commitment to you. If you're lucky, you may have an opportunity to repay her when she is old – when her body and mind are decaying and she needs someone to cook for her and change her diapers.

But the amazing thing about life is that in those moments when our mother fell short of giving us what we needed, someone else probably stepped in to do so. God,

Buddha or some Higher Power did a pretty good job of orchestrating our love. He just didn't want to give the entire responsibility to one person. So he delegated different pieces to different people at different moments. Ultimately the source of that love, regardless of what face we see when we open our eyes, comes from the same place. To be aware of the countless ways we have been loved throughout our life is to be aware of that source. And that awareness easily transcends the mistakes or human limitations of our birth mother. Or adopted mother. Or of any single human being.

So thank you, mom, for all those moments of loving care you provided. And thanks to the rest of the team, who carried out their respective roles at just the right time. I'm here, right now, thanks to all of you. Let's celebrate the spirit of motherhood – a spirit which reveals itself in the words and deeds of moms everywhere. You know who you are.

And sometimes . . . so do we.

..c Need Difficult People: Naikan on My Father

by Morris Sullivan

I hated my father. I had plenty of reasons for that. My father drank too much, too often, and his drinking often led to violence. When I was a child, I used to go to sleep at night praying that I wouldn't wake up in the middle of the night to the sound of him beating my mother.

When I was in elementary school, my mother somehow managed to make him stop whipping me with his belt, but she couldn't stop his verbal cruelty toward me. As if the physical and verbal violence toward my mother, brother and me wasn't enough, he also lied compulsively, had at least one affair and abused the family pets. By the time I entered high school, I had written him off as a role model. I dropped out of school before my senior year in order to make a living laying carpet during the day and playing in a rock band at night. I hoped to make enough money to move out of the house.

One night, I was sitting in a window booth in a coffee shop where my band hung out after gigs. My mother's car pulled into the parking lot, and I saw her get out and start for the door. I could tell she had been through a rough time. No doubt, she had managed to escape a beating and was out looking for me to tell me not to go home. I went outside to talk to her.

"Morris, I shot your father," she said. "But I didn't kill him."

"It's okay, mom," I answered. "I'm sure you tried."

Looking back, my mom and I can laugh about that. At the time, it wasn't funny. However, the marriage finally ended that night. She got a restraining order and never saw my father again. Since I was an adult, I could choose whether or not to visit him. I chose not to. For the next 12 years, I didn't see him and avoided his phone calls.

When my father found out I was married and had a child, he begged to see photos of his grandson. I still carried around a lot of anger toward him. I saw myself as a victim and my father as my victimizer. I blamed a lot of my own perceived inadequacies and social problems on the abuse I had suffered and the violence I had witnessed.

An encounter with Naikan and the process of self-reflection began a process of healing and transformation.

The Larger Story

I started studying Japanese psychology after I was inducted as a sensei (teacher) with the Bright Dawn Center for Oneness Buddhism. We had used Gregg Krech's Naikan book in our training program, and that rekindled my interest in Naikan, which had begun back then in the mid-1980s after I read a book by David K. Reynolds. His book described a Japanese method of self-reflection which used the three Naikan questions developed by Yoshimoto Ishin to examine one's relationships.

I had decided to ask the three Naikan questions about people in my life, starting with my mother, and then moving on to my father, examining my life in seven-year increments.

For several nights, I went through this process, sitting at the kitchen table and writing down my answers in a journal. I had no problem answering the three questions about my mother. We always had a good relationship and I saw her as very supportive. However, I hit a wall when I started on my father. I mostly wanted to focus on a fourth question: "What trouble did he cause me?" Naikan doesn't have us ask that question – most of us spend too much time on that question already. I had certainly been reliving dark moments from my past.

But despite my resistance, I did the exercise anyway, starting with the question, "What did I receive from my father?" Like it or not, I had received much from him, including life itself and half of my genetic makeup.

He had also taught me a lot of important things, like the basics of carpentry and electronics. He had grown up in a place and time where "do it yourself" wasn't trendy—it was a necessity. I'm no handyman, by any means, but thanks to him I can fix a toilet, dig a post-hole or paint a bedroom.

He was a very creative guy in a lot of ways, although he never put it to much use. He was the son of a hard-assed working man in rural Texas, and he was expected to work, too. My father spent too much time trying to make a living to be able to do anything too creative, but he encouraged my creativity.

He had played trombone in the high school band and encouraged my interest in music. When I wanted to be a musician, he agreed to forego luxuries so he and my mom could buy me a cherry-red Epiphone "batwing" electric guitar. He made sure I got guitar lessons and put up with the noisy practice sessions. Later, when I was in a glam band, he even defended what he called my "individualism" when other adults criticized my hair and fashion choices.

As I worked through that first question, I began to see him differently. As bad as he was, he wasn't entirely evil. My coldness started to warm . . . just a little bit.

Then I got to the second question, "What did I give my father?" I really didn't remember giving him very much for the first 14 years of my life. His acceptance of some of the gifts I'd given on birthdays and holidays was so ungracious it was painful to recall.

Then I remembered that he had loved hearing me play Creedence Clearwater Revival's "Bad Moon Rising." Sometimes when I was playing my guitar, he'd knock and come into my room, saying, "Play a little of that 'Bad Moon' for me, son." I didn't like the song all that much and didn't do anything special with it—just strummed the chords—but he'd sit on my bed and smile, and I'd play it through a couple of times for him. It felt good remembering those moments.

I also reflected on the problems I caused my Dad. I had to admit, I had not been particularly innocent—I had caused some pretty significant troubles. I tried to run away from home twice, and he drove all over town at night looking for me. Then he had to call the police and let them know he'd found me.

I began to learn meditation when I was about 13. One day, I brought home a giant ceremonial candle, which I burned in my room, hoping to meditate on the flame until I reached enlightenment. That didn't happen. However, I did leave a giant waxy circle of soot on the ceiling, which my father had to paint over three times before it was finally covered. I expected anger, but he laughed about it.

When I first learned to drive, I backed over a curb one night in my mom's '68 Impala and broke the exhaust manifold. I woke up the next morning with my father sitting on the edge of my bed. As I opened my eyes, he asked, "What's wrong with your mom's car?"

I braced myself. I thought he was going to be really upset. But after I told him what happened, he said that we'd go to the auto parts store after breakfast. We bought the part, and he showed me how to replace it. I think he actually enjoyed the time we spent together. My causing him trouble turned into another gift from him.

I Wanted to Stay Mad

Damn it! I really wanted to stay mad at him. But I just couldn't.

That weekend, I phoned him. He was surprised—and very happy—to hear from me. I sent him photos of my son and a family portrait. After that, we had a cordial relationship. My brother and I even went to Texas to visit him and stayed with him for a few days.

He came to Florida for a visit in 1988, and my brother and I took him and our sons out on a family excursion—just a day trip to a state park to do a little sightseeing. That night, I invited him to come to an open mic night at a local nightspot. I got a couple other members of my band to meet us there, and we went up and played a few songs—including "Bad Moon Rising."

My Dad died about 10 years later. I won't say we became buddies. My Dad wasn't Henry Fonda, and there was no rosy Hollywood ending. My father hadn't changed: He had been a violent drunk and, even with limited contact, I still saw that side of him from time to time. But that wasn't all he was.

Being able to see my relationship with him through the lens of Naikan changed my life in many ways. I was able to let go of something I had been holding onto very tightly—the burden of anger I had carried for so long.

That alone was freeing. But I also let go of the crutch of victimhood I'd embraced. When you can't rely on your usual excuses, you either have to accept your flaws as they are or free yourself from them.

Finally, the ability to have understanding and compassion for my father made it a lot easier for me to accept such faults in myself and others. I think I'm less self-righteous. My father wasn't all bad and I wasn't all blameless.

An eighth-century Buddhist monk called Shantideva gave a long teaching on compassion, and he pointed out that even Buddhas need non-Buddhas—we need difficult people to help us develop the wisdom and compassion we need for spiritual growth. Seeing that even a man like my father was capable of good things helped me develop compassion for other people. If I could find goodness in him, I could find goodness in just about anybody: even in myself, when the shadow of my father's darkness occasionally falls across my own face.

A Father's Heart

by Christina & Alexandra Newton

D*uring the ToDo Institute's annual self-reflection course in 2007, we were fortunate to have a father enrolled along with his two adult daughters who now had their own families. One of them, Alexandra, was living in Argentina. During the course, each of the adult daughters, Christina and Alexandra, posted their Naikan reflection about their father on his birthday. As they reflect on their father, we feel not only the sense of gratitude they have for the love their father offered to them as children, but we also get a sense of how this type of reflection can create an atmosphere of love and appreciation in a family. Instead of getting caught in a web of criticism and condemnation, we see and begin to truly appreciate the unique way that family members, particularly our parents, have made our lives possible. Here is Christina's reflection:*

Today, November 8th, is my father's birthday and I want to list some of life's moments that I have had with him that I cherish:

- The walks along the beach at night in Amagansett singing songs from Finnian's Rainbow;
- The camp outs we had under the stars in Vermont;
- The amazing canoe trip to the Finger Lakes. My love of nature comes from those times;
- Helping you with whatever chore;
- Weeding, cleaning out the apartments in Vermont, raking the endless leaves, re-caulking a window;
- You taught me to take care of my stuff and to do a little bit every day;
- You reading me Oscar Wilde;
- Taking me to the ballet;
- Going on trips all over the world on mom's standby airplane tickets, wanting us children to eat with you parents because you thought we were interesting;
- Thank you for instilling a desire in me to learn and read and discuss.

You being the first to come when my daughter, Carrie, was born 10 weeks early. The picture I have is your large hand holding her tiny one. Thank you for so often being there when I have needed to talk to you.

• For allowing your granddaughters come and stay with you during the weeks in the summer. Feeding them, talking to them, playing with them, letting them mess up your stuff. They have fond memories of their times in Vermont;

You called me the other day and apologized for not being there enough for me when I was a teenager. I want to thank you for the many, many times you have been there for me, as a baby, as a child, as a teenager, as a young woman, as a mother, through my divorce, and relationships and remarriage, I feel so blessed and there is no doubt that you are there for me and that is such a gift. I have recently learned that love and respect can never be demanded, they can only be given. Thank you for having given me so very much. As I write these memories I see anew the life of real privilege I have had because of you.

Thank you. I love you,
Christina

Now, here is Alexandra's reflection:

I thank my sister for sharing what our father has given her and inspiring me to write before his birthday ends.

• You have given me the name Pappi which I have always loved;
• You have given me your love of nature, our walks, always long ones, down the Sugarbush mountain in summer, skiing with you so quickly through the Glades of Sugarbush, trying to ski like you when I was eight and then suddenly one day, with your patience, my snow plow transformed into a beautiful vadle.
• You gave me your friend, Gerry, and the laughter of yodeling with him down the mountain;

40

- You gave me the cold of the mountain and how to endure what was difficult;
- You gave me two full days of skiing every weekend, all winter, with the long drive from New York City;
- You gave me sports – how I loved to learn golf with you, to walk on the golf course early in the morning when the dew was still there and we would see a rabbit. How I loved your golf clubs.
- You gave me the hours of playing tennis together in Vermont, and later when I lived in California, how wonderful it was to play with you.
- You gave me swimming – showing us how to love water, and your dives and flips were so beautiful. You gave me persistence as I raced in the Sugarbush Inn pool and could see you next to the pool cheering me on.
- You gave me the world of the piano – taking me to Mrs. Battista when I was seven for the first time and then buying me a different piano for every home we lived in.
- You gave me a way to organize my time on a sheet of white paper so that I could practice six hours a day in summer and two during the school year.
- You gave me my love of writing – reading to me first your father's stories from his brown leather bag and later your own.
- You gave me your mother Mama Licha and her dog Chamba whose independence was passed on to me.
- You gave me weekends alone with her on Bedford Street in the village when I was four and the basis of a friendship between grandmother and granddaughter that would grow stronger with the years.
- You gave me your companionship on the boat Minot's Light in the middle of the Baltic Sea when the first man landed on the moon and we toasted the moment.
- You gave me your love of dancing and how you loved to lead me when we danced together in our 81st Street apartment.
- You gave me your doubts and questions about how a marriage should be and today, when I felt sad and cried twice, I wanted to call you and be comforted by you. I intuited it would be better for the Naikan approach to thank the tears for appearing, feel the pain of the moment, receive another's hurtful words and not try to hurt

41

another back but really see the orange trees and the laundry I was taking off of the line which was something else you gave us – a clothes line you hung in Vermont.

- At our home, you built Nicky a tree house and we slept out doors in your green army sleeping bag and toasted marshmallows. You gave us the shooting stars as we sat on the deck at night.
- And the sound of the birches and pines in the wind – a sound that will always be my childhood.
- You gave me a beautiful crib you made out of wood for my dolls and the way you could make new walls and really make anything we needed.
- You gave us strength, creativity, the ability to make do with whatever you had.
- You gave us your hard work.
- You gave us your Mexican and British heritage and the desire in me to bridge both worlds.
- You gave me a brother and two sisters and I don't remember any fighting when we were little.
- You gave us a sense of being a team.
- You gave us your laughter and your loud sneezes and watchful eyes in all of my performances in Boston and the way your vision zoomed on me when I lost my finger on stage and didn't say ouch but finished the last moment of the play.
- You and Joyce cleaned every inch of our apartment.
- You gave me your companionship on the first day of Sarah Lawrence College and your interest in my courses.
- And then, in Iowa City, living alone and pregnant with my fourth child, and later with my family in Argentina trying to begin a doctorate, you gave me a sense of still being young and that everything was possible.

You have been a wonderful father, Pappi. I love you,

– Alexandra

Here is the father's response to Alexandra's Naikan . . .

Alexandra, Alita, my dear first born:

My God, talk about reflecting, your memories of our growing up together remind me of what an extraordinary life we have shared. With tears pouring down I read your tribute to me and to our many moments together. What great times we shared. And I thank you from the bottom of my heart for writing of our times together as it is sometimes so easy to forget what joy we have shared, and some pain too.

You know what I remember so well – that you were so tenacious in everything you did. The piano, schooling, skiing, and so much more. Thanks for reminding me of so much. I better go get another handkerchief.

Love,

Pappi

And to his youngest daughter, Christina,

One of the most rewarding aspects of this Naikan forum is its emphasis on reflections. My daughter, in her birthday thoughts of me has me reflecting on the joy which parenting can bring.

My little baby, now no longer a child, is always in my mind's eye – my little baby.

Your reflections on our many times together were wonderful.

I love you,

Dad

Failing to Make Payments

by Les MacFarlane

People describe Naikan in many different ways: Some call it self-reflection; some call it psychotherapy; others call it meditation. Whatever we choose to call it, this structured method of self-discovery helps us turn over rocks in our memory and discover the truth about our lives. Forgotten acts of kindness from others often surface as we reflect upon our relationships. I found this to be particularly true when I reflected on my Dad.

When I was growing up, Dad was a salesman for a large glass company in Toronto. As part of his job, he received tickets to local sporting events that were to be used to reward loyal customers or simply to develop business relationships with new customers. Occasionally, his customers were busy, and he would take me instead. Sitting in Exhibition Stadium on a warm May evening, watching the Toronto Blue Jays face off against the Yankees with a Coke and my Dad's companionship, is one of my fondest childhood memories.

So when my boss gave me a pair of tickets to see an Ottawa Senators hockey game, I knew immediately I would invite him. Actually, after doing Naikan on my Dad, I made a pact with myself that I would take him to a sporting event in every season. This Senators game would be my first chance in winter to make a chink in the debt I owed my father.

When I invited my Dad, he immediately said yes. A chance to go to a Senators game is not something he gets very often. When the night of the big game came, Dad picked me up at five o'clock. I asked if he wanted to come in so I could fix him something to eat. He shook his head and said he'd rather pick up something along the way. I thought he intended to pull into a fast food place or grab a hotdog at the game. Instead, he parked by a nice restaurant and told me that since I provided the tickets, he wanted to take me out to dinner. So I had a good meal, and Dad paid. Total bill: $35.

This repayment process wasn't going according to plan. So far, Dad had spent gas money and $35 on dinner, half of which was for me. After dinner, it was time for the game. We left early so we could see the pre-game activities. We pulled into the Corel Center and I discovered that parking cost $10. This was my first hockey game at the center, and I was unaware we had to pay for parking. I generally carry very little cash with me unless I'm planning to make a specific purchase—I find it cuts down on frivolous spending. So I only had three dollars in my pockets—just enough for a soda at the game. Dad pulled out a ten dollar bill and paid the attendant without even looking at me or asking.

I said, "Here—take this," offering the change I had.

Dad said, "No, no. You got the tickets. I'll do this."

So to recap: I got free tickets, and at this point, my father had spent $45. I was deeper in debt than when I started out. I would never be able to repay him at this rate.

I believe, however, there are good reasons to continue to try to repay the people and things in our lives for the support we have received. For me, repaying these debts is what needs doing. And I believe feelings can provide information. I feel guilty about how much my father has done for me and how little I have given in return. That guilt is pointing toward action. So I express gratitude—that's what needs doing.

In Naikan: Gratitude, Grace, and the Art of Self-Reflection, Gregg Krech articulates this point succinctly:

"Whether we can actually repay our debt, and avoid increasing it, can only be determined by our sincere effort. The effort itself may lead to the realization that our debt to others can never be repaid. But until we have exhausted ourselves trying, we won't know, nor can we comprehend, the grace that underlies the fabric of our lives."

The second reason for attempting to repay others is that it requires a shift of attention from ourselves to others. As we make this shift more completely, we lose our self-focus. When I think of people who inspire me, I think of people like St. John Bosco, Gandhi and Thich Nhat Hanh. These people spent their lives shifting their attention from their own needs to the needs of others. It seems to me they lived admirable lives. I believe this shift from self to other is a big part of that.

Dad and I walked into the Corel Center. At one point, I looked at him and saw him smiling as we walked toward our seats in Section 21, Row R. We were at Row A, and began climbing the stairs to Rows B, C, D, going higher and higher. By row J, I felt we should have been given a Sherpa guide to help us with the final ascent. Row R was the very top row!

My Dad looked at me and smiled. "You got these from your boss for your performance at work?" he joked, gesturing toward the lower rows. "If I were you, I would be wondering if there are a whole lot of your coworkers down there."

We both laughed. We watched the game. The Senators won.

Dad dropped me off at home afterward. I offered to pay him back for dinner and the parking. He told me to never mind—if I hadn't gotten the tickets, he couldn't have gone. He thanked me for the tickets and drove away as I went into the house.

It was just like when I was a kid. I had a great day, and my Dad had taken care of everything. I think the only difference is that now I am a little older, a little more aware, and a great deal more grateful.

My Life in Cars
by Gregg Krech

A central theme in my relationship with my father was cars. It started, of course, further back than I can remember. I was driven around as a young child to family gatherings, doctor's appointments, restaurants, and school. I didn't get very far as a child without wheels, and those wheels were paid for and often driven by my dad.

At 16, I obstinately decided I was going to have my own wheels – no more sharing a car with my parents. I had saved some money and found a 1967 green Mercury Cougar that was "cool" looking. It would have been a great car judged on looks alone, but its ability to get me from one place to another was severely hampered by a dysfunctional engine.

Twice, I blew a head gasket (major engine problem) while going with my girlfriend on excursions out of the city. Each time Dad showed up with his own car and a rented tow-bar to pull me home. Both rescue trips required about two hours of travel each way. And after each breakdown, he arranged for the mechanic at his workplace to repair the engine at minimal cost.

When I graduated high school, my dad bought me a used Toyota Corolla as a gift. That got me through my college years. I subsequently moved to Washington, D.C., and my dad offered a sizable down payment on a brand-new Toyota Celica.

Now that I was young, single and working, you would expect the car legacy to end, but it didn't. At age 25 I had major knee surgery, and my full leg cast couldn't deal with the clutch in my manual transmission Celica. My dad drove his own Buick from Chicago to Virginia and traded cars with me for six months. When my knee heeled, he drove the Celica to Cleveland from Chicago. I was visiting my girlfriend's parents in Pittsburgh, so it was an easy drive to meet him there and reclaim my sporty car again.

After 10 years, my Celica was ready for retirement. My eye caught sight of a car just recently introduced in the U.S. – the Acura (made by Honda). I bought a new Acura Integra, and once again my Dad came up with the down payment that made it possible.

In 1992, I moved to Vermont and got married. My Acura was still healthy, but my wife owned an ailing Toyota Corolla that wasn't going to survive New England winters and dirt roads. I found a used all-wheel-drive Subaru near my old home in Virginia. My dad lent us the money, and we traded the Corolla to a local service station for a good pair of snow tires. We paid my dad back (at no interest) just in time to get a new loan from him on a new Subaru in 1995. We were now a two-Subaru family.

By the time we were adopting our first daughter, it was time to retire the older Subaru and get something "safe" for our child to ride in. My dad and I agreed that a used Volvo was the way to go – they were like tanks. He spotted a 1992 Volvo Station Wagon in a parking lot at a commuter train station in Chicago. He had it inspected, negotiated the sale, arranged for some minor repairs, and then drove it from Chicago to Vermont. He delivered it to our home about nine days after we returned from China with our baby girl, Chani. The car came with another personal loan, and the Kia Minivan that followed, to accommodate a second child and a rescue dog, came with a down payment from him.

I acquired my driver's license on my 16th birthday, and ever since my Dad has made the transition to the next car just a bit easier. Whether it was a down payment, a loan or door-to-door delivery, I can't look back at a single vehicle that doesn't somehow bear his stamp of generosity. Oh – and I almost forgot – he also taught me how to drive.

Thanks, Dad.

Naikan and Conflict Resolution

by Linda Anderson Krech

Naikan can be a powerful tool for reconciliation. Sometimes I keep this tool in my back pocket or even walk around with it in my hand, but that's just about useless. If I take it out and use it in a focused and wholehearted way, it can be transformative, revealing missing pieces that may dramatically change what I see and understand.

Many years ago, a group of family members and I helped to start a center in New York for those with serious mental illness. Fueled by a passionate desire to help our loved ones and a great disappointment in the existing mental health system, we secured funds, found a space, hired a director (who then hired me as his assistant) and opened the doors. It was a dream come true.

The director, however, was not living up to my expectations. On the second day of the program, he did not come in, choosing instead to attend to non-urgent personal business. I had been watching his job performance with some dismay during the preceding months as we prepared to open, noticing all the things he could be doing that he was not doing and becoming increasingly disappointed. When he didn't show up on the second day, I was livid.

The next day I communicated to him, in front of other staff, that I thought he wasn't doing his job and that I was concerned about whether he could succeed in this position (remember, he was my boss!). Needless to say, things were very disrupted by this confrontation, and I wondered where it would lead. That night, not knowing what else to do, I did Naikan reflection on him. Not feeling like it, I took an hour and reflected on Naikan's three simple questions.

What had I received from him?
What did I give to him?
What troubles and difficulties had I caused him?

What rose to the top of my awareness was all that he had done to move us

49

forward with this beloved project — tasks I would have had trouble doing and didn't enjoy doing. I realized the effort he made that enabled us to open our doors. And I recognized specific troubles that accompanied my being on his staff, not the least of which was my ongoing scrutiny of his performance.

Before work the next day, I bought him some flowers and left them with a note on his desk. The note said something like "Thank you for all you've done to get us to this point. I hope we can work together to make this an extraordinary center." When I saw him hours later, he could not speak. He was very emotional and indicated that he would talk to me later. Then I found a note on my desk that said, "That was one of the kindest gifts I have ever received."

Naikan's influence is softening. It opens the heart, redirects the attention, helps us to mind our own business, and allows us to get unstuck. Naikan helped the two of us strengthen our partnership. What could have been the beginning of the end instead became the beginning of a better relationship for us. I got busy doing my job rather than monitoring his; he got busy making extra room in his life for the huge demands of his position. Maybe we could have found our way there without Naikan, but I don't think so. He remained the director of this program for more than 20 years and the program was a phenomenal success under his leadership.

I invite you to consider using Naikan when you are caught up in conflict with others. It's worth a try. It may help you to make wiser decisions, ones that you will not regret, decisions that are more fair and open-hearted. It may help you put yourself in the other person's shoes. The world could use a bit more of that right now.

Naikan and Neighbors
by Zoe Weil

For many years, a neighbor plowed our driveway. After a few years, he raised the price a couple of dollars, and the following year he raised it a few more. I was a bit put off that we didn't discuss the annual increase, and I brought it up with him. He said that if I could find someone to plow cheaper, I should have someone else do it. I was a bit embarrassed and responded that I just wanted to know if the increase would be several dollars each year. Over the next few years, he didn't raise the price, although his cost for fuel certainly went up during that time.

During the week in which I was reading Gregg Krech's book on Naikan, I was awakened one morning at 5 a.m. by the sound of my neighbor plowing my driveway. It hit me like a ton of bricks: For 8 years, my elderly neighbor had been getting up in the wee hours of the morning in all sorts of weather while I'd been snug in my bed. He had been making it possible for my family to come and go in the midst of winter storms. A couple of weeks later, when I got my bill for that month's plowing I wrote my neighbor a long-overdue thank you letter and let him know I'd be increasing what I pay him by $5 per plowing, starting with the check I enclosed. I felt so much better about the relationship after that.

After a few more years, my neighbor let me know that he was no longer going to be plowing. Not only was I unable to find anyone to plow for any less money than I was paying him, I was never able to find anyone else who did nearly as good a job.

Grandfather and the Siberian Winter

by Andy Bienkowski

One of my most vivid childhood memories is from Siberia, where, at the age of six, my family and I were banished by the Russians. It was in the winter of 1940. The section of Poland where I lived had been taken over by the Russians who deported over one million Polish citizens to Siberia. The deported Poles, including my family, were deemed undesirable citizens of the new Soviet territory and so were cast out. We were dumped unceremoniously into the Siberian countryside to die of starvation, disease or cold. There were five of us: my mother, my younger brother, my grandparents, and myself. Father, who was an officer in the Polish Army, fought against the German invasion. He was captured by the Russians and held as a prisoner-of-war, so he was not with us.

Great suffering surrounded us. Many people froze to death or died of various diseases related to the extreme cold, malnutrition, and close quarters. There were entire days when we had no food at all. We were slowly starving to death. One day, my grandfather decided (quite consciously) that he was not going to eat any more. He explained to us that as a result of his decision, there would be more food for the children – my brother and me. Even though the family disapproved, he was very firm and stuck to his decision. As I remember, it took him about two weeks to actually die of starvation.

This made quite an impression in the mind of a 6-year-old, and has been an inspiration for the rest of my life. My grandfather's last wish before he died was that we should bury him without his clothes, so that we could sell his clothes to buy food. That winter was very cold and the ground was frozen. We buried him in a shallow grave in the prairie. When we returned to visit his grave, his body was gone and there was evidence that he had been eaten by wolves.

My experience in Siberia and my grandfather's death shaped my own philosophy of life. I have always had trouble with the "me first" attitude which dominates our culture and is publicized in so many self-help books. This philosophy does nothing to nourish your soul. In the end, it only makes you feel selfish. A life of service, on the other hand, will ultimately enrich and give meaning to your life.

Meeting Grandmother for the First Time – Again

by Kathy Abromeit

I met my grandmother for the first time – again – while doing Naikan at a Benedictine Monastery. My grandmother was born in 1888 and lived to the ripe age of 95. Her first husband died in a freak accident, and the second husband walked out, leaving her with five young children to raise.

As an unskilled woman with a lot of mouths to feed, she was in a terrible situation. She saw herself as having two options: prostitution or bootlegging. Both of these would have allowed her to make a livable wage in a short period of time, so she could still care for her children. She picked bootlegging. She explained it this way, "There was honor in bootlegging."

She referred to herself as a "distributor," carrying the bottles of corn whiskey on ropes under her long dresses. She was in jail a few times and knew Al Capone's brother, who was the primary bootlegger in northern Idaho. After prohibition, she owned a little restaurant in town and died in 1983 when I was a 21-year-old junior in college.

I took a photo of my grandmother with me to the hermitage, as well as some jewelry she had given me and a rosary I had purchased for her at the Vatican when I was 16 years old. I also found a wool jacket she had given me long ago. I wore the now snug-fitting jacket throughout much of the retreat.

My reflection on my grandmother was divided into six sessions to be spread over three days, with the first session focusing on my relationship with her from birth to age nine. Each session thereafter focused on three-year periods. The final session was used to write either a letter or poem of gratitude for Gramma. The length of time for each Naikan session varied slightly, ranging from 50-90 minutes long. After a few sessions, I started to feel like I was bearing witness to the pixelated parts of a larger image, and it was exciting to watch the whole picture unfold.

I had never done Naikan so intensely on a specific relationship from beginning to end in such a focused period of time. I was struck by the simplicity and innocence of the harm I caused in those early years, recalling things like sneaking behind her garage and eating raspberries off the vine, cutting through her garden as a shortcut through the neighborhood, or making a mess in her bathroom as I did some sort of chemistry experiment with various bath products.

It got more complicated as I got older, and I noticed that my harm became more laden with self-absorption, anger and ignorance. I found myself noting how my fear of the death process, and her death in particular, prohibited me from spending much money on phone calls to her while I was in college. I know she missed having more regular contact with me, as I did with her. My inability to remain present with her as she died made me miss the opportunity to give witness to her life as well as receive her final gifts.

It was interesting to do Naikan reflection on a person who has died. The relationship was in the "past," yet it was being cherished in the "now" with all the life experiences and journeys that have brought me to this moment. Through this retreat, I gained a sense of the interconnection of past, present, and future. I am grateful to have had this transformative "first experience," again, with my grandmother.

Thanking Mom

by Peter Smithfield

*I*n 1999, Peter participated in an online course on Naikan reflection with the ToDo Institute. During that time he reflected on a number of his relationships, including his relationship with his mother. He wrote the following essay, describing how this reflection impacted on his relationship with her.

Last summer, due to economic circumstances, I lived with my mother and father. I was very nervous about this. The majority of the time my mother did not want me to live at home, and I rarely wanted to live there myself. Just to put things in context, my mother is an alcoholic and addict; as I was growing up, she was a rabid feminist who hated men and yet was utterly dependent on them at the same time. I am just as stubborn in many ways. I don't put up with a lot of nonsense from her, and neither does she from me.

In June, I began doing daily Naikan reflection on my relationship with my mother, going year by year, circumstance by circumstance. I was absolutely amazed by the generosity of my mother throughout my life. My former therapy taught me to hate her and blame my problems on her. Yet with Naikan, I saw a very scared woman who constantly gave and gave at her own expense. Who changed a thousand poopy diapers and nursed me through all kinds of illnesses. And in myself, I saw a kid, a teenager, and a man who did nothing but take and complain and inconvenience her.

I sent her a thank you card and an abbreviated list of the things she had done for me. This really freaked her out, and she ended up complaining about it to my dad. I believe it scared her, because it was completely out of character for me to do something like that for her. But I just kept thanking her when I saw her, told her I loved her, and hugged her. Somewhere around July, our relationship started blooming like a flower. She calls me to tell me she loves and misses me. I call her and send her letters. Did it solve all our differences? No. We are still apples and oranges. But now, I get to go home for Christmas to a mom who loves me, trusts me a little bit more and lets me talk to her about our lives.

Swimming in
Turbulent Waters

> *"The most fundamental aggression to ourselves, the most fundamental harm we can do to ourselves, is to remain ignorant by not having the courage and the respect to look at ourselves honestly and gently."*
>
> – Pema Chodron

Introduction
by Gregg Krech

"Examine life outside the boundaries of your suffering."

Whether we are facing a life-threatening illness, a home that has burned to the ground or the disappointment of not getting a promotion, life continues to push us up against our edge. In the film, *Manchester by the Sea*, we see a character, Lee Chandler, who is continuously pushed beyond his ability to cope with his circumstances. Like many of us, he has moments when he rises to the occasion, and, moments when he lashes out in anger or retreats to the deceptive comfort of alcohol.

Regardless of our circumstances, when we are suffering most, we are least inclined to step back and reflect on our lives. Our mind and heart (*kokoro* in Japanese) is too preoccupied with its own suffering to consider any broader understanding of our situation. We live with questions that arise from self-pity like steam rising from a hearty stew: *Why me? How could he do this to me? Why is life such a struggle? Why is life so hard for me?*

59

And we respond as if we were alone: *I can't do this. I can't cope anymore. It's too hard. It's too much. Nobody understands. Nobody cares.*

In such moments we may find a small crack in our cell of suffering which lets in some light and lets us see the world around us. Like a bear waking from hibernation, we may be able to open our eyes to a world that is offering more than just pain. A world that also offers kindness. A world that offers moments of humor, or even joy. We are hungry to find a supportive and caring vision of the world, yet a part of us is also reluctant to give up the security of our suffering. We can cling to suffering like an old piece of clothing that fails to offer warmth or beauty, yet fits us so well.

In Naikan retreats, participants have an opportunity to reflect on a difficult situation from their past. It may be a divorce, a struggle with disease, an accident, a betrayal by someone they trusted, or the death of a loved one. Such an exercise is never assigned, only offered. We need to be ready to confront the painful episodes of our past and that readiness is something that only we can assess. Once we're ready, what does self-reflection offer us?

First, it offers us the extraordinary opportunity to discover the foundation of caring and kindness that helped us get through our difficulties. We did not survive through our own efforts. Someone helped us change the flat tire. Someone provided medical advice. Cars, roads and gas offered us transportation.

As a result of an injury in 2015, I struggled with chronic pain for about six months. The pain started in my neck, through my left shoulder and down into my arm where 3-4 of my fingers were constantly tingling. I found it nearly impossible to sleep, because as soon as I shifted my body in bed, the pain would wake me up. Yet, throughout this period of time, a collective of people, objects and energy was working to support me. There were medical professionals like chiropractors and physical therapists. There was a car that got me safely to and from appointments on roads that were maintained so I could drive. There was nourishing food, supplements and pain medication that eased my distress. There were movies that distracted me and heat and ice packs applied to alleviate pressure on the nerve. There was the internet which offered an endless opportunity to research undiscovered treatments. There was even an inflatable neck pump, purchased through Amazon and delivered by a UPS driver, which allowed me to gradually stretch my neck and temporarily reduce the degree of pain.

In other words, while I was suffering, the world was working toward making that suffering more bearable and even attempting to alleviate it. When we are suffering it is difficult to notice the care which is being offered, and even more difficult to genuinely appreciate it. Self-reflection is a portal that makes this perspective more accessible.

In traditional Western mental health, there is frequently an underlying assumption that to be cured from our past suffering we have to express it, let it out. It is a kind of exorcism in which the demon (past suffering) who possesses us can, through the proper ritual, be evicted from our mind and heart. I would like to offer another perspective on what it means to be cured, to be healed.

We are incapable of evicting any of our karma, pleasant or painful, from what we have become. If we have suffered, we have suffered. That suffering becomes a part of us. To be cured is a function of two essential ingredients: Acceptance of ourselves and our karma — not only the suffering we have had to bear, but also the suffering we have imposed on others. And secondly, the recognition that, despite our transgressions, our selfish acts and the problems we have caused, we are loved. Our suffering is understood in the context of love. We are loved not because of how we have lived, but despite how we have lived. This is nothing less than the recognition of grace in our lives. And this awareness is, in itself, grace.

Over the Edge—
In Search of Perspective on Tragedy
by Melissa Ericksen Cocuzza

In August 1986, I was in an accident. I was 25 years old at the time. I was 4 ½ months pregnant and I had an ideal pregnancy up until that day. I didn't eat breakfast before I left for work, since I usually ate when I arrived at work. I went to commute on the Long Island Railroad and was in a good position on the platform to get a seat, which meant I was on the edge of the platform, so I would have been one of the first people to board the train.

That morning I felt an odd chill, which was very strange since it was 101 degrees out. I remember thinking, "Should I stay where I am or go to the back of the crowd and sit down?" I looked at my watch and saw the train was due in only two minutes, so I decided to stay where I was. That was my last memory until I awoke in the emergency room with a team of doctors and nurses all busy about me, preparing to cut off the rest of my clothes.

I reflected on this event during my Naikan retreat in 2003. Here is a statement of my reflection as I looked back on my accident and the period just after it occurred:

What Did I Receive?
- The train conductor made an emergency stop;
- I heard that someone had jumped onto the tracks to be with me;
- Emergency workers assisted at the scene, then made a good decision to make sure I went to a decent hospital, out of their jurisdiction;
- The emergency room staff evaluated my condition and determined the care I needed;
- The oral surgeon replanted my teeth and set my broken jaw bone;
- The plastic surgeon closed a big wound on my chin;
- The orthopedic staff helped reset my arm broken in six places;
- Others cared for my fractured ribs;

- Medical staff monitored my concussion;
- My cousin arrived first and was allowed to come to me and stay for a while;
- Someone called my husband to let him know, and provide the information he needed;
- My family members called other family members;
- My mother came down from Vermont to Long Island;
- My loved ones decided that even though I was in the critical care unit in the maternity area, I should have round the clock care, so they hired a private duty nurse to be at my side for at least two nights that I remember (it made me feel better knowing I wasn't alone);
- I received some visitors, although I don't remember much;
- When I was out of the critical care unit, I had a roommate so I had some company;
- During my eleven days in the hospital, I received the nurses' daily care, and care from specialists who treated me and monitored my progress;
- People washed my bedding and administered my medicines;
- There was heat in the building, electricity for all the monitoring devices and lighting;
- A bed to lie in;
- Food given through an intravenous feeding unit;
- My OB/GYN monitored my expected baby, and the sonogram person checked on my baby;
- The ambulance and its technology provided assistance en route to the hospital;
- Blankets to keep me warm;
- Gowns to wear, as my clothes were cut off me and no longer usable;
- My mother comforted me and reassured me that I would be okay, but she recommended I not look in a mirror yet.
- On the fourth day I asked again, "Can I look in the mirror yet?" Mom said now it would be okay. When I looked in the mirror, I didn't recognize myself at all. Still, the fact that my mother conveyed her unconditional love when I was that scary-looking is pure love;

- My husband Jerry knew what would cheer me up and make me feel better during my long recovery – my sister. As a surprise, he arranged to fly her in from California. She arrived with a nurse's hat she had made from a Chinese food container. It said MASH 4077, because she was here to help me mash my food, as my jaw was going to be wired shut for over a month, and I was restricted to bed rest for one month, as well;
- Others did my laundry, grocery shopping, helped care for Jerry emotionally, and probably helped also with his food, laundry and cleaning;
- My sister and others shuttled me to many follow up doctor appointments;
- It was months before it was determined that I fainted due to my pregnancy, so for that period of time I was driven anywhere I needed to go;
- I received a call from my uncle that he missed me, but he didn't feel up to coming to get me, and would I come see him if he sent a cab? I said yes. He took me to an upscale shopping area that I could not really afford, and when we passed a fancy maternity shop he said, "Do you have an outfit for the upcoming holidays?" I didn't, and he asked if I liked the one in the window. I said it was very nice and he said, "Lets go in." The salesperson asked if she could help, and he said, "We'd like the outfit on display for my niece." She gathered the items and he bought them. We then proceeded to a lovely lunch in an expensive restaurant. It was a beautiful, intimate time with my uncle, which had never happened before. My uncle died, unexpectedly, two days later;
- I received many flower arrangements and get well cards;
- My two bosses came out to Queens from their homes in Manhattan (half an hour's travel) to tell me in person, on behalf of the company, "We don't want you to even think of money. We will pay you your full salary until the baby is born" (which was another 4 $^{1/2}$ months' time)
- My husband did not think of himself at all during this time; everything was geared to me and the expected baby's wellbeing;
- Sometimes when I was lonely my aunt and sister-in-law would come and pick me up to visit with them and then return me home later;

What Did I Give?

- My verbal thanks to those assisting me;
- I wrote thank you notes to the police officers who responded, the train conductor and his supervisors, and the ambulance crew that made the decision to take me out of their jurisdiction to see that I received better care;
- I also dropped off large boxes of Godiva chocolates to the police and ambulance people;
- I wrote to the person who I was told jumped onto the train tracks to be with me;

What Troubles & Difficulties Did I Cause Others?

- I caused all the commuters on the Long Island Rail Road to be late to where they were going, and perhaps to explain their late arrival to their bosses. I delayed and disrupted the schedule for the day;
- Maybe the ambulance crew took some heat for their decision to take me to the better hospital and not where they would normally go;
- I also knew from others who were on the train that the conductor announced, "There's something ahead on the tracks – I'm going to make an emergency stop," so everyone had a strong jolt due to the sudden stop;
- I happened to meet a man, months later, who recognized me, and he asked me how I was. During that conversation, I asked him what happened, and he said, "I never screamed so loud." So, I apparently caused fear in him and probably others;
- I guess I was bloody and scary looking too, which may have upset others;
- The ambulance crew probably got worked up knowing someone needed their help. Also, they had to adjust the care they normally would have provided because of my pregnancy;
- Since I could not receive any pain medicines, they probably were more considerate of the treatment they provided;
- My husband left his job to be at my side;
- My mom left her job for days to be with me;

- My sister left her job for days to be with me;
- Those who left their jobs for hours, or days, may have lost wages;
- The hospital staff cared for me;
- My husband did not have me available to cook his meals or do his laundry;
- Others prepared my drinks and blended my foods;
- Others cleaned my house, my bedding and did my shopping for several months;
- Others drove me to doctor's appointments and waited for me, then drove me home;
- My appearance probably disturbed some people when I went out to the doctor visits;
- My family and friends were probably upset to see me in such poor shape.

After the accident, when I had recovered enough, I asked myself the question, "Why did this happen?" I didn't think it was fair. I realized that there is a time for each of us. I realized that it just wasn't my time. I no longer live with a fear of death – when it is time, it is time.

My Naikan reflection on this accident has allowed me to see, in detail, all the thoughtful acts that were done on my behalf by other-many efforts by my family and people with whom I had never even spoken. At a time when I was wounded, weak and unable to care for myself, people were there for me, watching over me, offering their love and support to help me get well. It renewed my faith in the world that we are intrinsically good, and it awaked my deep gratitude. I am more clearly aware now of my obligation to do for others.

Postscript: I am now 41 years old. I live a relatively normal life. I am in some type of back or neck discomfort every day, although I continue to seek new medical avenues and have learned and developed skills to live fully while in some discomfort. My son was born healthy and uninjured by the accident. I named him Jeremy after my Uncle Jerry, who had died during my pregnancy. He is now 16 years old.

Finding Freedom in Prison
by Carol O'Dowd

I recently made an unplanned trip to Indonesia to help my son, who has been living there for the past 10 years. He made a grave mistake of having marijuana in his belongings. For a mother, it was heartbreaking to watch events close in around my only son such that he might be separated from his children. Traveling to a totally different culture and navigating a foreign system of laws as a family representative proved to be even more difficult. The mornings were filled with squawking chickens and barking dogs that roamed the courtyard. Getting through a day without language skills and no translator was disorienting. I felt isolated and trapped by events. At times, it felt like I, too, was in prison.

As events unfolded in the legal system, it became obvious that I lacked the ability to influence – much less control – any event in this situation. My response was to sink into a state of loss, pain and fear that limited my ability to respond to much of anything, including outreach emails from friends. At the time, it was difficult to understand that even though events and conditions were not to my liking, the freedom to choose how to respond still existed.

One evening, using the three questions of Naikan to reflect, my focus slowly shifted to something other than the destructive emotions of anger, frustration, and even self-loathing for not being able to provide much help. Slowly, I began to see how my behaviors were part of the problem, and that helped reveal ways to connect, rather than to remain isolated. I could only do my best, and then trust what followed to the flow of life.

My son was being held in Kerobakan prison, where most of the prisoners are incarcerated for drug-related offenses. Inside the prison, a small Buddhist temple sat empty. I am a Shin Buddhist; I'm also a certified Mindfulness Instructor and Addiction Counselor trained in the Buddhist-inspired practice of Naikan. At the request of some prisoners and with approval of the director of prison programs, a few inmates and I made efforts to reactivate the Buddhist temple. We used it to share simple practices for dealing with difficult situations. The prisoners cleaned the room, contributed oscillating fans and donated cushions. Several of them constructed a koi pond next to the temple.

With a cool space in the tropical heat and the sound of flowing water to mask outside conversation, we practiced mindfulness with chanting, meditation and Naikan reflection. The prisoners in Kerobakan demonstrated how to discover freedom, whether confined inside a concrete jail cell or trapped within the walls of painful emotions. These men were models for how, in the midst of even extreme challenges, it is possible to shift from anger and loss to a focus on making a positive difference.

Using Naikan as a basis for change during one session, prisoners explored the second Naikan question, "What did I give to others?" When I asked if anyone had anything to share, a prisoner responded with, "I gave tears," explaining he had been in a fight. After explaining that the question means, "What gifts they had given?" the prisoner said, "I gave nothing to anyone all week."

Suddenly, the prisoner behind him slapped him on the back, with a loud, "Not true! You gave me a bowl of soup last week." A smile spread across the man's face and laughter erupted from everyone in the room.

Some prisoners began to look for opportunities during the week to give to others. During the Naikan sessions, prisoners began sharing how they gave gifts of smiles, safe places to sit for a while, and food to a stray cat that had wandered into the prison yard, along with giving time to help clean equipment and assisting with tasks such as gardening.

Prisoners learned how to recognize gifts they received, as well as what they gave to others and what behaviors caused troubles for others. Several prisoners attempted to shift a behavior pattern of automatically throwing a punch when angry to pausing to consider whether starting a fight would help or cause more difficulties.

Inmates who came together to explore living mindfully taught me how we all have been conditioned to respond to events and circumstances by our respective families, cultures and upbringing. We discussed how automatic emotional responses can restrict us within the bars of an emotional prison that can be stronger than those of a prison cell. By reflecting upon actions and words, prisoners began to see some of the choices they were making. They considered how freedom exists to make a conscious choice rather than an automatic preconditioned emotional response, no matter the situation.

Such a lesson is useful for anyone who is trapped in the prison of emotional responses, whether they live in an institutional prison or in their own home. By listening with the senses and reflecting upon our actions and words, we can choose how to respond instead of being led around by destructive emotions.

After several months in Indonesia, my journey to help my son and deal with my experience of being confined by emotions has taken me, too, to a place of greater freedom. We are looking forward to mt son being reunited with his children and working again, hopefully in a matter of months.

As I write, I am planning for my return to the United States. Some of the prisoners and I plan to stay in touch as they are released. For those with long-term sentences, I will provide support via email. Having formed a non-profit, we hope to continue to share Naikan and other valuable practices that can help all prisoners find freedom.

What Will Come Next?

By Otavio Lilla

On Monday, as I was driving home for lunch with my brother, we stopped at a traffic light behind a small truck. Suddenly, a distracted man came down the street with his nice, brand-new car and crashed into our car, pushing us under the truck in front of us. My car was almost totally destroyed, but nothing happened to us. As I stepped out of my car to talk to this man, who was about 65 years old, he took off. I was totally amazed that someone could leave an accident scene like this without even caring whether or not someone was hurt.

Fortunately, people on the street witnessed the accident and noted his license plate. These people helped us pull the car over to the side, so as not to create a problem for the traffic. They also testified at the police department.

Then people came to tow our car to the repair center. They did all the work— I just had to phone and wait. My brother helped me bring home the items that were inside the car. The police officer in the police station was very kind and helpful. My aunt even offered to lend me a car while my own was being repaired (if it could be repaired). This made my life much easier during the next several weeks. Everyone was kind and helpful.

Most importantly, we were incredibly lucky to not get hurt in this accident. I was so grateful to be alive and well and grateful that my brother was also alive and well. No one was really injured. My life could have been fatally interrupted at that moment, even though I was only waiting for a traffic light to turn green. All my future plans, my relationships, everything, could have been ended by this sudden, unexpected event.

I realized again that positive circumstances cannot be taken for granted and that things can turn very bad sometimes. I think if it had happened in a different moment of my life, before the practice of Naikan, I would have been angry, bemoaning my bad luck. Life cannot be taken for granted—not even the next breath. They say we do not know what will come next: death or the next breath. This is so true.

Naikan and Illness
by Kara Jacobs

I've found Naikan is most useful in those situations which repeatedly lead me to create my own little cloud of self-pity and resentment.

For example, almost seven years post-chemotherapy, I am one of the few people who have sustained permanent damage to my bone marrow: my bone marrow is unable to produce sufficient red blood cells, leading to a specialized type of anemia. The treatment consists of shots of a human growth factor to stimulate the bone marrow to make these cells. Now, you might think I would be grateful to be alive, receiving these shots and otherwise in good health . . . and I am. But I can also easily work myself up into a fit of anger and resentment.

Why me? Why do I have to be the one in a million this happens to? None of my other cancer buddies have to do this! I hate returning to the infusion center, where I get my treatment! I'll have to do this for the rest of my life! It's not fair! I'm permanently damaged! I get so tired! Nobody understands how I suffer!

So when I came in for my shot, I decided to do Naikan on my situation. Here is my reflection:

What Have I Received?
- I am alive to receive this treatment;
- I am alive to receive this treatment because my mother gave birth to me and my parents nurtured and protected me;
- I am alive to receive this treatment because a surgeon was able to remove my cancer;
- I am able to walk, talk, think, see, and breathe without pain;
- There are trees for me to see, and flowers, and fish, and spider webs, and so much more;
- My car brings me to the appointment;
- My medical insurance pays for most of this expensive treatment, and my partner

pays a monthly amount to co-cover me on his insurance and that pays most of the rest;

- My job allows me the flexibility to take time off to come in every month;
- There are magazines and a puzzle and comfortable seats in the waiting room, and bottled water and hot water for tea and coffee as well;
- The technician skillfully inserts a needle into my needle-wary vein, wraps my arm in my choice of colored gauze;
- A computer miraculously outputs the results in minutes, the nurse smiles at me, takes my blood pressure, and answers my questions;
- I am the beneficiary of this marvelous medication, and all the research that went into developing it;
- I am treated in pleasant, clean surroundings with sterile equipment;
- The nurse covers the site of my shot with a Bugs Bunny patterned Band-Aid and gives me a calendar with my future appointments on it;
- A receptionist uses her computer to schedule the appointments;
- Someone has left little handmade pillows in a basket for patients to take home with them if they so choose;
- Somebody built the stairs, which I now take down to the floor level of the building;
- The parking lot is paved and easily accessible;
- My oncologist received training and knowledge from many centuries of observation, research, and experience, and in turn passes on the benefit of this expertise to me;
- The traffic lights help me navigate safely to the appointment.

What Trouble I Caused?
- I use up valuable resources (gasoline) to get to my appointment, no doubt causing some pollution on the way;
- I contribute to the wear and tear on the highway and roads;
- I contribute to the congestion on the freeway and may have slowed somebody down;
- I take up a parking spot rather near the entrance, thus occupying a space that somebody who is more disabled than me needs more than I do;

- I also take up a chair in the oncology waiting room, as well as time and resources for my care that might serve other people;
- I create extra work for my doctor, the receptionists, the technicians, and the nurses, and also for the people who process my insurance claims; my partner worries about me;
- My partner has to pay extra to cover my care;
- My care may contribute to raising the rates of others in my medical group;
- My doctor is somewhat perplexed and upset that my bone marrow still has not regenerated;
- I am not at work while I'm doing this, meaning I am not readily available to my clients for this period of time;
- My supervisor may have to deal with a crisis on my caseload because I am not available for this period of time;
- I am creating trash (Band-Aid, needles, etc.) which uses up resources and which others have to attend to;
- Other patients may feel bad because I am relatively healthy, have all my hair, can walk, and am generally doing well, thus serving as a living reminder that life is not always fair.

What I Gave:
- I suspect that the staff enjoys seeing someone come in who looks healthy and is doing well overall;
- I see my favorite nurse from the old chemo days and give her a hug;
- I'm contributing to job security for more than one person;
- Perhaps being on the receiving end of services makes me a better, more compassionate social worker (so this is really something that I have been given, too!);
- I chat and laugh with an elderly gentleman in the waiting room, and I believe this cheers him up and helps him pass the time;
- I am gathering information for a short essay on "Emergency Naikan," which might actually inspire somebody else to do their very own Naikan intervention!

Peasant Marey

by Fyodor Dostoevsky (1821–1881)

Allll these *professions de foi* are, I think, boring to read. So I will tell an anecdote, actually not even an anecdote-only a very old, distant recollection, which, for some reason I very much want to tell, precisely here and now, in conclusion of our treatise about the people. I was only nine years old at the time. But no, I had better start with what happened when I was twenty-nine years old.

It was the second day of Holy Week. There was warmth in the air, the sky was blue, the sun stood high, "warm," bright, but in my heart it was very gloomy. I was wandering around behind the barracks. I looked at and counted the posts of the prison's stockade fence, but I did not really feel like counting them, although it was my habit to do that. It was already the second day of "feasting" in the prison. The prisoners were not convoyed out to work, there were many drunks, there was swearing, fights were breaking out everywhere all the time. Ugly, disgusting songs were sung, card games and gambling were going on under the bunks. A few prisoners, beaten half dead by the prisoners' own court, for especially violent misdeeds, lay on the bunks, covered by sheepskin coats, till they would regain consciousness and wake up. Knives had been drawn several times. All this, after two days of Easter, upset me till I felt sick. I was never able to endure without disgust the people's drunken debauchery, and particularly not here, in this place. During those days, even the authorities did not search the prison and did not look for liquor, understanding that, once a year, even these outcasts must be allowed to kick up their heels, otherwise things would become even worse. Finally I flared up in anger. I happened to meet the Pole M_____tski,– one of the political prisoners. He looked at me somberly, his eyes darkened, and his lips trembled. He gritted his teeth, said in a low voice, "Je hais ces brigands!" (I hate these brigands), and walked past me.

I went back into the barracks, despite the fact that fifteen minutes before I had run out of them like someone half demented when six healthy, strong peasants had thrown themselves, all at the same time, on the drunken Tartar, Gazin, in order to quiet him down, and had beaten him up. They beat him horrendously; one could have killed a camel with blows like that. But they knew that it was hard to kill that Hercules, and so they beat him without pulling their punches. Now, when I returned, I noticed Gazin, unconscious, at the end of the barracks, on the bunk in the corner, giving no signs of life. He lay there covered by a sheepskin coat. Everybody was walking around him in silence. They were firmly hoping that the next day towards morning he would come to, "but from blows like that, one never knows, a man could even die." I made my way to my place across from the window with iron bars, and lay there, face down, put my hands behind my head, and closed my eyes. I liked to lie like that. People leave you alone when you are sleeping, and you can dream and think. But I was not able to dream. My heart beat restlessly. In my ears I heard M_____tski's words, "Je hai's ces brigands!" Anyway, what is the point of describing my impressions? Even now I dream of that time, at night, and those are the most agonizing of all my dreams. Perhaps my readers have noticed that until today, I have not once spoken in print about my life in prison. I wrote "Notes from the House of the Dead" fifteen years ago as if narrated by a fictional character, a criminal who was supposed to have murdered his wife. As a matter of fact, I will add this detail, since that time many people think about me and even now assert that I was sent into exile for the murder of my wife.

Bit by bit, I really did sink into unconsciousness and gradually became submerged in reminiscences. In the entire four years of my imprisonment I recalled uninterruptedly my entire past. It seems that in my memories I lived again through all my previous life. These recollections came of themselves. I seldom called them forth because I wanted to myself. It began from some point, some trait, sometimes an unnoticeable one, and then little by little it grew into an entire picture, into some strong and whole impression. I would analyze those impressions, add new traits to what I had experienced a long time before, and, most important, I corrected it. I corrected it ceaselessly; that was what all my pleasure consisted of.

This time suddenly an insignificant moment from my earliest childhood, when

I was only ten years old, came into my memory. A moment, it would seem, which I had completely forgotten. But at that time I loved especially memories from my very earliest childhood. I recalled August in our village, a dry and clear day, but somewhat cold and windy. The summer was drawing to its close, and soon we would have to go to Moscow, to be bored again all winter doing French lessons, and I felt so sorry to leave the country that I went out past the barns, and down into the ravine. I walked up to Losk; that was what we called the thick shrubs between the other side of the ravine and the woods. I pushed further into the bushes and I heard, as though from nearby, thirty steps away, in a clearing, one of our peasants, who was ploughing. I knew he was ploughing on a steep slope, and his horse was walking with difficulty. From time to time his shouts reached me, "Nu, nu!" I knew almost all our peasants. But I did not know which of them it was who was ploughing there. It was all the same to me; I was all preoccupied with what I was doing. I was busy, too. I was breaking off a twig from a nut-tree with which to whip frogs. Whips out of nut-tree twigs are so beautiful and elastic, much more so than birch tree ones. I was also paying attention to bugs and beetles. I collected them; there are some very beautiful ones. I also liked small, nimble, reddish-yellow lizards, with black spots, but I was afraid of snakes. Actually one ran across snakes much less often than lizards.

There were few mushrooms there. One must go in the birch woods to find mushrooms, and I was planning to go there. There was nothing in my life that I loved as much as the woods with their mushrooms and wild berries, with their little bugs and birds, porcupines, squirrels with their humid smell of rotting leaves, which I was especially fond of. And even now, as I am writing this, I can smell the birch woods in our countryside. These impressions remain with one all one's life.

Suddenly, in the middle of the deep silence, I heard clearly and distinctly the shout: "There is a wolf!" I cried out. Beside myself with fear, shouting out loud, I ran into the clearing, directly to a peasant who was ploughing there.

It was our peasant Marey. I don't know if such a name exists, but everybody called him Marey. He was a fifty-year-old, thick-set, strapping peasant, with a lot of grey in his brown, broad, thick beard. I knew him, but before then I had almost never entered into a conversation with him. When he heard my cry, he stopped his horse, and when I ran up and seized his plough with one hand and his sleeve with the other, he realized how frightened I was.

"There is a wolf!" I shouted, out of breath.

He lifted up his head and involuntarily looked around. For a moment he almost believed me.

"Where is the wolf?"

"Somebody shouted... somebody just now shouted, 'There is a wolf!'" I babbled.

"Come on, come on, what wolf? It just seemed to you like that. What kind of wolf would be here?" he muttered, cheering me up. But I was shaking all over and held on to his coat even more firmly. I must have been very pale. He looked at me with a worried smile, evidently fearing for me and worrying.

"Oh, so you got scared, oh my," he shook his head. "Enough, my boy. No, no, boykin."

He reached out and suddenly stroked my cheek: "Enough, now, Christ be with you, cross yourself."

But I did not cross myself. The corners of my lips trembled, and it seemed that this particularly struck him. He reached out with his thick finger, slowly, and touched my shaking lips very quietly with his black finger-nail soiled with the earth. "Now, now, oh," he smiled at me with a kind of motherly, long smile, "Oh lord, what is this all about, oh come on, now."

Finally I understood that there was no wolf, and that I had only imagined that someone had shouted "wolf." The shout had really been very clear and distinct, but I had imagined such shouts (and not only about wolves) once or twice previously, and I was aware of that. (Later, after I grew out of childhood, these hallucinations disappeared.)

"Well, I'll go now," I said, looking at him questioningly and timidly."

"You go, and I will watch you. I'm not going to let the wolf get you," he added, still smiling in the same motherly way. "So Christ be with you, go, go now." He made the sign of the cross over me with his hand and crossed himself too. I went, looking back almost every ten steps. Marey stood next to his horse and looked at me as long as I was walking away. He nodded to me every time I looked around. I felt a little ashamed before him, I must confess, for having been so frightened, but I walked on, still very afraid of the wolf, until I had walked up the slope of the ravine, to the first barn. There my fright dropped off altogether and there our dog Volchok [Little Wolf] appeared, out of nowhere, and jumped up at me. In Volchok's company, I cheered up completely, and turned towards Marey for one last time. I could no longer make out his face clearly, but I felt that he was still smiling at me tenderly in exactly the same way as before and that he was nodding to me. I waved to him with my hand; he waved to me also, and moved his horse along.

"Well, well," I heard him shouting in the distance. His horse was again pulling the plough.

All this arose at once in my memory, I don't know why, but in astonishingly precise detail. I regained consciousness suddenly and sat up on the bunk. I remember there was still a quiet smile of remembrance on my face. I went on reminiscing for another minute.

When I came home after having met Marey, that time, I did not tell anyone about my "adventure." What kind of adventure had it been anyway? I even very quickly forgot about Marey. Later I met him seldom. I never even talked with him, about the wolf or about anything else either.

Now suddenly, twenty years later, in Siberia, I recalled our meeting with such absolute clarity, down to the last detail. It means it had sunk down into my mind imperceptibly, all by itself, without my wanting this. And suddenly this meeting was recalled when it was needed. That tender, motherly smile of a poor serf was recalled, and the peasant, his signs of the cross, his nods, his "Oh well, boy, how frightened you are." And especially his thick finger dirtied with earth, with which he quietly, timidly, tenderly touched my shaking lips. Of course anybody would have cheered up a small boy, but that time in this isolated meeting it was as if something quite different took place. If I had been his own son, he could not have given me a look shining with clearer love. Who was forcing him to do it? He was a peasant serf who belonged to us, and I was his young master. Nobody would know how he comforted me, and nobody would reward him for it. Did he love little children so much? There are people like that. Our meeting took place in isolation, in an empty field. Perhaps only God saw from above the deep and enlightened human feeling and delicate, almost womanly tenderness which can fill the heart of a coarse, bestially ignorant Russian peasant serf. He was not expecting or guessing at that time that he would be freed... Tell me, was it not this that Constantine Aksakov understood when he spoke of the high education of our people? And when I got off the bunk and looked around me, I remember that I suddenly felt that I could look at those unhappy people with an altogether different attitude and that suddenly, through some miracle, all hatred and anger had disappeared from my heart. I walked on and looked deep into the faces I encountered. This peasant, his head shaved, dishonored, his face branded, drunk, roaring out his drunken, sleazy song, perhaps he is that same Marey. I cannot see into his heart. That evening I met again M_____tski, too. Unhappy man! He could not have any memories of any Mareys. He could have no opinion of these people other than "Je hais ces brigands." No, these Poles suffered more than we did!

"Peasant Marey" was published for the first time in the February 1876 issue of the journal Diary of a Writer, which Fyodor Dostoevsky wrote, edited, and published single-handedly, cover to cover.

Reflecting on Occasion

*Sometimes I go
about in pity for
myself,
and all the while
a great wind is bearing me
across the sky*

– Ojibwa (Native American) Saying

Introduction
by Gregg Krech

When we reflect on our life in whole or part, we generally don't see it as one flowing, sequential film. More commonly, we watch it in scenes. Many of those scenes tend to be events or special occasions – some pleasant, and some not so pleasant.

The scenes which stand out in our memory can include trips, holidays, weddings, funerals, birthdays, surgeries, graduations, accidents, moving to a new home or city, layoffs, and more. As with a scene in a play or film, we arbitrarily mark the beginning and ending point. In real life, one moment flows into the next. But in our memory, our vacation ends when we arrive home, unlock the door and our Golden Retriever barks and gets excited.

We often label the scenes of our lives as good or bad. Our minds prefer the black and white version of reality. It's less confusing and allows us to avoid trying to understand a world of various shade and hues, some of which conflict with others. But in most of the good scenes there are unpleasant experiences and moments. And in many of the "bad" scenes there are redeeming qualities of that experience in which we learned something, received love and support from others, or deepened our sense of faith or humility.

When we reflect on a past scene or period of time using Naikan reflection, we are taking the opportunity to see the experience through a different lens:

Were there ways that I was cared for and things I received that I'm leaving out of my understanding of the scene? Is there something I'm missing?

Were there ways that I helped or gave to others that I haven't considered in my understanding of the scene? Is there something I'm missing?

If I consider others who were part of the scene, can I see ways that I've caused them trouble or suffering? Can I try to understand their experience and what it was like dealing with me in that situation?

Sometimes when we reflect on the past, an experience that caused us great distress can become humorous – simply by the insertion of time. The pain fades, like a fog lifting, and we are able to see the humor or irony of the situation.

When my daughters were ages five and seven, my older daughter approached her sister and grabbed a toy she wanted from her sister's hand in a rude and aggressive way. I happened to see it so I marched over to my seven-year old and said, "If you want something, ask for it politely, don't just grab it." And then I angrily grabbed the toy from her hand and gave it back to her sister. At the time I was genuinely angry, but by the next day I was able to laugh at my own hypocrisy.

The power of self-reflection offers an opportunity to shift the energy of a scene. For example, anxiety has the capacity to color almost any occasion. If you are genuinely worried about what might happen, you have little awareness of what else might be going on.

In March, Vermont was hit with a major snowstorm that dropped 30+ inches of snow on us over a two-day period starting on a Tuesday morning. On Thursday night of that week, my oldest daughter, Chani, and I had tickets to see a professional hockey game in Ottawa, Canada – about five hours away. The tickets had been my

Christmas gift to her and we had made arrangements to stay in Ottawa, visiting friends, for three days. But the unexpected snowstorm cast doubt on whether we would be able to travel and get there in time. My daughter had been looking forward to the trip for months, but as the thick snow blanketed our area without pause, we realized that we might not be able to get out and get there in time. In the morning we would go outside and shovel a foot of snow and by evening we were outside shoveling another foot. We worried about losing electricity so we gathered flashlights and kept a fire in the wood stove since the furnace required electricity. Our friend, Tracy, who reliably plows our driveway, came three times with his pickup truck, and had run out of room to put the snow. The snow dissipated on Wednesday night, but we went to bed wondering whether the roads in northern Vermont and across the border in Canada would be passable on Thursday morning.

They were.

The road crews must have been out all night long plowing and sanding the roads, even as gusts of wind blew the snow back on to the roads. Both the Vermont and Canadian road crews did an extraordinary job of making the roads safe for travel. As we drove, we saw cars and trucks that had run off the highway and had turned over in the snow, presumably the previous night or hours earlier. But with our all-wheel drive Toyota and good snow tires, we made it to Ottawa without incident, arriving earlier than we expected. We attended the hockey game, saw friends, and created a wonderful father-daughter memory.

In the aftermath of the trip, once the anxiety had vanished, I was able to reflect on the experience and understand how fortunate we had been and how many people and objects made it possible for us to travel. There were dozens, perhaps hundreds, of road crew employees that worked with little or no sleep to make the roads passable. There were huge plows and trucks and mechanics that kept them maintained. There were weather forecasters that warned us in advance of the storm, and people who had trucked sand in months ago from great distances. There was Tracy, who plowed our 500-foot driveway, allowing us to get down to the dirt road. There were people who kept the electricity on so that stoplights were functioning. The car we drove was well-designed and well-maintained by local mechanics. The snow tires had been mounted and properly balanced. We had a full tank of gas. The Canadian customs agent allowed us to cross the border. And while we were gone, our home was heated, phone messages were recorded, and the food we left in the refrigerator remained cold.

A scene originally experienced with the energy of anxiety was remembered with a sincere sense of gratitude and good fortune. We will never relive the actual experience. The experience of the moment is here and then gone. It is the memory of the experience that we carry forward – for days, months or years. It would be a disservice to reality to allow the feeling of anxiety to overshadow all the people, objects and forms of energy that supported us.

Of course, not every scene has a happy ending. But in almost any scene, we can find love and support if we step back and reflect on it. And in most scenes, if we are honest, we will see our own contribution to whatever problems or difficulties arose.

At the end of our lives, we will have a collection of memories. Perhaps we'll have a chance to share that collection with someone we love. Perhaps not. But how we remember the scenes from our life will shape whether we die feeling grateful for having lived, or, whether we die holding on to resentment, anger and self-pity. Our capacity to reflect on the scenes of our life will do much to color our last thought, our last feeling, and our last breath.

An Afternoon With Yo-Yo Ma and Everyone Who Wasn't There

by Margaret McKenzie

L ast year, I purchased season tickets for the Chicago Symphony Orchestra. Three of us travel from the Chicago suburbs to the city about once a month. We attend concerts with violin and piano soloists, brass ensembles and full orchestra accompanied by a chorus. Once we even heard a contemporary piece that included a broom and a typewriter. But the most sublime moment of the season took place the last week in May, when Yo-Yo Ma joined the orchestra to perform the Schumann Cello Concerto in A Minor.

I own CDs of Ma and have seen him on television and on film. I had no idea what a difference it would make to experience his performance in person. The energy he brings to the stage is palpable. The connection between him and his cello is organic; it appears to be an extension of his body. The full attention that he gives to every detail of the performance is observable.

During the slow, quiet second movement, there was a period where only Ma and the first cello played and the rest of the orchestra faded into the background. As the duo played, I had the sense of seeing/hearing a ribbon of music flowing from one to the other. Whenever Ma was not playing, he leaned nearly out of his chair toward the other player. Though I was five floors above the musicians, I felt that they were right in front of me, playing just for me. We use the word "transcendent" much too freely these days, but this was that kind of moment. Something about space and time briefly disappeared.

When the concert was over and we got back on the train I reflected on the beauty and grace of that afternoon. I began, as Thich Nhat Hanh suggests, to look more deeply into all the people, objects and money that had made that moment of transcendence possible. What did I pay, and what value did I receive? If I bring the lens of Naikan to the day's experience, what do I find?

87

First, there was the train that carried me back and forth to the city, which I rode for free—in Chicago, seniors ride free. Then there was the ticket: one of a season series of eight, it cost about $45 for that performance. My friend Ginger actually handled the transaction online and purchased the tickets. All I did was write her a check and appear at her door.

Next, there is the hall where the concert was held. Designed in 1904 by famed architect Daniel Burnham, the hall is designated a National Historic Landmark and was renovated in the late '90s for $110 million. My $45 got me a seat in a landmark building where the acoustics are impeccable.

Next came the concert itself. The playbill I carried home with me made it possible to see many of the contributions that made that performance possible. We could start with money first – twenty-three pages of the booklet are devoted to the names of individuals, foundations and corporations that donated to the symphony. Corporations I think of as only profit-driven had contributed a half million dollars each. There are also thousands of individual donors. How remarkable that thousands of individual people decided to take a portion of their income and donate it for my listening pleasure.

Looking deeper, there is the gift of time. The entire governing and fundraising committees of the orchestra are composed of volunteers. The ushers are volunteers. And the orchestra members volunteer their time to be a part of the youth education program. The whole orchestra donated the performance the following night to benefit a pension fund.

Then there are the musicians. Behind the musicians sit the parents, who drove each of the 100 members of the orchestra to thousands of hours of music lessons; who purchased instruments and hundreds of music books. You find the teachers who instructed and encouraged them, along with the people who came to their first concert when they were ten years old and cheered them on. Six musicians were interviewed in the playbill. When asked about their first teacher, they said "I started piano lessons with my mother at age 5" (two people said this). "I got my first flute at age eleven through a public school program." Ma began learning the cello from his father when he was four. Asked about their most important influences, musicians replied "My parents who were constantly listening to fine music" and "the New York poet Kenneth Koch took me under his wing and many wonderful collaborations followed."

Then there are the instruments themselves. Looking deeply into Ma's cello, you discover a man in a workshop in Italy. It's three hundred years ago, and he is patiently working the cured Italian spruce to form the body of a cello. A cello which is now so valuable that it is owned by a foundation that lends it to Yo-Yo Ma. A cello that will eventually bring a taste of eternity to a spring afternoon in Chicago.

During the concert I can simply immerse myself in the music and the orchestra as they are in this very moment. But when I reflect on the "roots" of this experience, I realize what a miracle it is for this event to take place—and what a gift it was to be in the audience that day.

Mind the Gap

by Jane Palmer

In England there is a charming expression, "Mind the Gap," that appears on signs throughout the subway system and refers to the treacherous space between the platform and the train. "The gap" is definitely NOT a place you want to step into. I took the title of this essay from another place we don't want to be—the gap between our reality and our ideal of what it should have been. I found myself there a couple of weeks ago—it wasn't fun, but it was juicy. I wanted to share with you what happened, because you might find yourself there someday, too.

"This gap between reality and our ideal of what life should be like attracts our attention like a magnet" (Krech). Sometimes, the gap can be so vivid and compelling that it becomes the whole story, to the exclusion of everything else. I caught myself in the gap over the Christmas holiday, when my son was home from college.

This is my smart, tender, wonderful son, whom I love like life itself. He also can be, shall we say, a bit messy. I examined the kitchen like a sergeant on inspection duty, scanning the countertops for evidence of Sam's misdeeds: a dirty pan, milk left out to spoil. God forbid! I was actively looking for discrepancies to be aggravated about, which was stupid. I don't love it when he leaves a mess in the kitchen, but when our time together is limited and there's so much that's good, does it really matter?

Unfortunately, it's possible to make a habit out of this kind of gap-minding. How many of us go about our days focused on how reality fails to meet our image of the ideal: the ideal partner, ideal son or daughter, ideal outcome? I used to do this with my husband. I'd think, "Damn it, why can't he be more outgoing? Why can't he be taller?" It's as if I'm entitled to the perfect form, which is nothing more than a fantasy. Then I get cranky when life doesn't deliver. It's a guaranteed formula for disappointment, disillusionment, even depression. We really don't want to go there. The problem is the expectation of the ideal – the clinging to fantasy at the expense of what's real.

Some expectations are what we could call aspirational — like planning to lose 10 pounds in the next month. Others are realistic expectations that don't get met when people let you down, when friends disappoint, when bosses offer false promises. These can be real heartbreakers.

Sometimes the gap is really no one's fault – just a gap between what we hope for and what really happens – a simple twist of fate.

The Big Party

I had a big birthday coming up, and decided to make a big deal of it. I wanted a bash. I wanted a crowd of people who loved me and would say wonderful, heartwarming things about me. The people I love from one facet of my life would meet and fall in love with the people I love from other facets of my life, and the whole thing would come together—this was my fantasy—in a sort of Festival of Jane. 75 people said they would come. We cooked three different kinds of chili, including vegetarian. We cleaned and moved the furniture around to make room for everyone, because in my house, a crowd of 75 was going to be a squeeze. We bought heavy-duty paper plates, quarts of salsa and the Sterno cans to keep the food warm. We bathed and blow-dried the dogs. We borrowed air mattresses because people were coming from New York, Connecticut, Philadelphia, Boston and Washington DC. I was so excited.

The party was scheduled for December 19th, which also happened to be the day of the Great I-95 Snowstorm. The phone started to ring at about 10 a.m. One by one, throughout the day, people called to say they couldn't come.

At first I was baffled. I'd been cooking and painting my nails, not listening to the weather report! Also, I'm from Michigan and tend to be a little macho about the weather.

I was feeling disappointed that my friends were such wimps. The phone kept ringing as the snow kept falling —all day long. Eventually, I came to see that it was a pretty big snowstorm and people had good reason to avoid traveling. But at the time I saw the day as a long, drawn-out string of disappointments. By the time the party

91

started, I was not at my best.

Did I mention that about 30 people were there? Yet for a long, miserable period of time, all I could think about was my disappointment that 45 more people weren't there.

The rooms where we had pushed the furniture to the edges looked empty to me, and there was so much food!

I felt jilted.

I'm a little self-conscious about telling this story. It reveals my true self-absorbed brattiness and the fact that I'm just a couple of spilled milks short of a kid having a tantrum at Walmart. But the experience of falling into that wretched little gap was so intense that even while wallowing in self-pity I thought, "I can find some meaning in this."

The obvious take-away is gratitude. I'm a fan. Gratitude is a miracle cure that works every time, and we'd all be much happier if we counted our blessings.

At the party, I was so busy feeling sorry for myself that I almost missed the presence of 30 wonderful, dear friends right here in my cozy house on the snowiest night of the year. I became grateful for the wisdom of those who did not come — some people actually died on the roads that night. And I was thankful for the graciousness of those who called to express their regrets.

But the little worm of disappointment was still with me. Gratitude works wonders, but it wasn't enough, and I didn't have time to get Buddhist. This was an emergency.

So I turned to a practice called Naikan, a method of self-reflection involving three questions. The first question: "What did I receive and from whom?"

For starters, 30 people gave me their celebratory presence. Specifically...

1. My daughter Alex had been home from college all week, helping with the preparations and painting the front door red because I wanted a red front door. She is, without a doubt, the most wonderful daughter a person could have.

2. My best friend of 30 years had skipped two days of work and driven down from Boston on Friday so she could be with me all weekend to help.

3. My other best friend had cooked gallons of chili verde and hired her son to videotape the party.

4. My son and his girlfriend had driven through the night, leaving upstate New York at 2 a.m. on Saturday morning when Sam got off work and arriving just as the snow started to fall at 6 a.m.

5. My cousin had flown standby from California, and taken a train from the airport to Philadelphia, and a bus from Philadelphia to Reading—about 30 hours travel time.

6. A couple who live in the hilly part of Reading had hitched a ride with someone with four-wheel drive.

7. Another couple, not young, had walked 1 ½ miles in the snow. They arrived with red cheeks and a still-warm loaf of olive-studded corn bread to go with the chili. I could go on.

The second Naikan question: "What have I given?"

1. I gave a party — for myself, yes, but also for my friends.
2. I made my house beautiful and loaded up the table with wonderful food.
3. I introduced people to others I thought they would like.
4. I made up cozy beds for my girlfriend and my cousin.
5. I offered everyone a great brunch on Sunday morning.

This is an interesting kind of reconciliation process, practical and spiritual. I started out thinking I'd been really generous, but after asking myself this second question I had a more realistic sense of humility. A lot of what I "gave" were things designed to reflect back on me, and there was also a lot I didn't give.

Which brings me to the third and most difficult question: "What troubles and difficulties have I caused?"

I spent a lot of energy noticing that 45 people didn't come to my party. But did I notice that I might be the source of trouble to others?

1. Didn't I shortchange the people who were there, welcoming them with less than a full measure of enthusiasm because my spirits were dampened by a series of events over which they had no control?
2. Didn't I stress out the people who called by letting them hear in my voice a trace of rebuke?
3. Did I even think about canceling the party? Never. I carried on like a bulldozer, expecting that things would happen just as I planned.
4. Have I ever let someone down by not coming to their special event? You bet I have. And remembering that piece of history was the final kick in getting past the disappointment and closing the gap. Only when we realize that we, too, are perfectly capable of doing whatever it was that we were so upset about can we come down right.

Those three Naikan questions work like a charm—like gratitude 911. What did I receive? What did I give? What trouble did I cause? They give me a more realistic view not just of myself but of the give and take that occurs in my relationships. It's so easy to take the efforts of others for granted, and to either inflate or minimize our own roles. We hurry through the day not noticing all the "little" facets of the interdependent web. But the little things aren't really little; they just seem so because we're being supported and can afford not to pay attention.

By actually taking note of what we receive from another person, we see the reality of how we are supported. By taking note of what we have given, we see the balance sheet. And by taking note of the trouble we cause, we get that last, sobering dose of humility and compassion. It's a good way to get over the gap when snow falls on your birthday. It's a good way to know the grace by which we live.

A Real Day of Atonement

by Barbara Sarah

It was past the halfway point of the Naikan Retreat in Virginia. I was sitting in an open closet. The poignant story of my life that I had expected to project on the wall – a black and white, '50s foreign-style movie, had not appeared. Rather, for four days I had been struggling to remember those still photo images from my past that would assist me in recalling the many gifts that had supported me throughout my life.

I had finally learned to report my reflections properly, answering the three Naikan questions without going off into long explanatory narratives that were originally meant to accompany the aforementioned film, possibly a personal La Dolce Vita.

Then came the day when we were asked to consider our history of lying and stealing. By the time I had reached the period of reflecting on my adolescence, I realized that for the first time in my life I was actually facing myself and the numerous transgressions I had committed throughout my life.

It dawned on me that for over forty years I had attended services on the Jewish High Holidays, and when it was time on Yom Kippur, the Day of Atonement, to confess my sins with the rest of the community, I always thought that those words in the prayer book were for someone else's wrongdoings. Me – arrogant, bigoted, cynical? Me – deceitful, egotistical, greedy, jealous? It must be others who were obstinate, possessive, rancorous and selfish. They must be the ones who yielded to temptation, were lustful or malicious.

And in that closet I saw myself for who I had been, for what I had done, for the many people I had hurt and disrespected, for a litany of wrongdoings, for years of stealing, lying and cheating. And so I requested that I not be brought food. In the tradition of my religion I fasted to purify myself and become clean. Until that day, my life had been a Grand Illusion and it was time to look into the corners of my memory and acknowledge my misdeeds and transgressions.

That afternoon I went into the bathroom, and when I looked at myself in the

95

mirror, I found the following words on an index card:

"We have seen the hard, argumentative, selfish mind which prefers to condemn and judge others rather than open itself to truth. The ego mind which will stop at nothing to see itself as "right" and "victimized." The mind of high self-image which justifies and rationalizes any behavior. But there are moments when this ego self gives way to something else. What shall we call it?"

I was certain that card had been left there for me, although I was sharing that bathroom with five others. (At last, one moment of self-focus that was useful!) By the time I had gone through my day of fasting and atonement – truly a "day of awe" – I knew that the jig was up. A light had gone on in my mind that could not be extinguished. I realized that not only must I replace my past orientation with a "new" mind, but that the realistic view that I had of myself and my behavior had stimulated a healthy and necessary guilt that would guide my future actions.

For many years following that retreat I have gone to High Holiday services and taken my rightful place alongside the other transgressors in the community. In fact, I don't have to wait for that once-a-year opportunity – I can examine myself at any time. My new mind and new behaviors guide my daily life, keeping things in perspective and helping me to express the gratitude I experience every day for having received these lessons.

The Move

by Victoria Register-Freeman

I was introduced to Naikan in the late 1980's. In the 30+ years since I made my first three-columned sheet, I have used Naikan both casually and intensively. Even in the casual years, I have tried to set aside some holiday meditation time to reflect on what-had transpired during the past year. This exercise kept me from writing one of those frighteningly cheerful holiday letters that seem to be clogging my mailbox.

Although I have none of the verifiable data points TED presenters are so fond of invoking, I believe that Naikan reflection has saved both my mental health AND my tooth enamel. I grind my teeth when I am stressed and I am usually stressed when I have not looked at all sides of a situation. Naikan gives me the wide view as opposed to the narrowly obsessive one that seems to be my default.

In 2014 I was looking forward to my end-of-the-year Naikan worksheet as having a bursting middle column. Things I had given. Due to a bizarre real estate closing that required a complete and sudden downsizing, I watched four moving vans pull out with the furniture I had donated to a non-profit for terminally ill children. Master gardeners came to my front yard and dug out the 50 day lilies for the Heritage Garden. Other master gardeners came and removed fountains, concrete cherubs, plastic worm bins, rain barrels, pots, even wrought iron gates. Neighbors came with wheelbarrows to remove vintage bricks and overgrown herb gardens. One strong, quasi-homeless man cheerfully removed a concrete cat no one else had been able to budge. My life of the past decade disappeared in 96 hours. It felt like Brigadoon, the mythic community that appears and disappears.

It was only after I walked through my totally empty former home and stood on the porch looking for the last time at the great river that flowed past it that it hit me how I had benefited from the flowing wave of folks who had removed items so efficiently. Until that point I had totally focused on what I was giving up. I had wrapped myself in the cloak of Lady Bountiful. It wasn't a good fit.

I entered into a world of reflection. Had I caused problems by asking everyone to come so quickly? Yes. Had I created awkwardness when I shrieked at someone who was about to pull up the wrong piece of wrought iron? Yes. Had I produced enough boxes for the folks to clean out the basement? No. Had I promised the same antique sign to two different people? Yes. Was my supply of Mountain Dew sufficient for the moving men? No. Did I dress in black all four days thereby depressing my neighbors? Yes. And there were quite a few more entries in the Problems I Caused column.

The heft of my middle Naikan column diminished. My Lady Bountiful image shriveled. True, I had given away lots of STUFF, things that would convert into cash for good causes, but I had been given something priceless....the time and talent of some good folks....movers, appraisers, handy men, neighbors, gardeners and gleaners. And if one does not think that talent is required to empty a three-story bed and breakfast in 96 hours, one should view the video of a 300-pound antique icebox descending a narrow, winding staircase.

Naikan reflection always helps me see life's balance. If I shine the spotlight only on my contributions, then the illusion of imbalance outshines reality. The seesaw of justice puts my derriere right on the ground and I succumb to the paralysis of a false analysis. Naikan gets me moving mentally again. This time in the right direction.

Reflecting on a Semester at Sea
by Michele Faris

This past fall, I sailed aboard the MV World Odyssey serving in the position of psychologist for 560 students and about 40 staff members under the banner of Semester At Sea. We sailed to 12 countries in three continents. During our time together, we formed a very close-knit community as we processed what it had been like to be in countries that were very different from the United States. In-country travel for our students included home stays with locals (such as Bedouins in Morocco, a Tostan village in Senegal or a family in Cusco, Peru.) We toured ancient ruins in Greece, traveled the slave route across the Atlantic and visited banana plantations in Ecuador. Other students engaged in volunteer work for turtle conservation in Costa Rica and Habitat for Humanity in Trinidad. We wrestled with many feelings ranging from gratitude to guilt as we observed how people survive and thrive in places such as a mental hospital in Barcelona, a favela (shantytown) in Brazil, or face homelessness in Athens.

It was my first time in all of these countries and so I had no experience to insulate me from the shock of observing extreme poverty for the first time. I was very grateful to have a regular Naikan practice and daily mindfulness of Naikan principles to anchor me in real life. It was helpful to reflect on the ship's crew, who took care of our every need. I was aware of how I was serving my clients and also how I troubled others, including Rick, my partner and traveling companion, who kept track of my schedule and our travel plans. Such awareness reduced my anxiety and helped me keep my wandering attention in check.

When it came time to disembark in San Diego, I was asked to speak to our entire community about "reverse culture shock." After giving it some thought, I decided that the best way to approach dealing with the predictable depression that comes with reentry into the United States, would be to share the basic principles of Naikan. I asked the students to envision the faces of all the people who had helped them complete this voyage – from parents to doctors, scholarship funders, the ship's crew, their professors, etc.

I asked them to extend this gratitude to people they met throughout their travels as well, including the people who may have confused, annoyed or hurt them because these people were also important teachers. Then we reflected on ways they may have served through volunteer opportunities in various countries. Finally, I asked them to consider the size of their footprint as they moved from country to country and also on the ship. Had they used ship resources responsibly? Had they been respectful as they visited other countries? Were there people to whom they needed to make amends? The audience was asked to consider these questions as they viewed them on a very large screen of beautiful slides a colleague had generously prepared.

I suggested to our students that this practice could provide a useful antidote to becoming overly self-focused as we return home to our affluent lives during a holiday season that is often so consumer driven. After my brief presentation, the students' attention was focused on a flurry of preparations for disembarkation. Later, many students found me in the crowd to express their gratitude for the chance to participate in our brief reflection together.

I hope that Naikan practice will provide our students with a sense of groundedness and purpose as they move forward with their lives, and I am grateful to have had the opportunity to pass on a practice that has sustained me for a good number of years.

Did You Get What You Deserved Last Year?

by Clark Chilson

I do not know about you, but I definitely did not get all I deserved this past year. If I had, things would have been worse. I came to this felicitous realization by reflecting on the year in a different way.

At year's end in the past, I used to conduct an annual self-sabotaging ritual. It consisted of documenting in a diary and ruminating on the Grand Canyon-size gap between what I wanted to accomplish and what I actually did over the previous 12 months. This led to my mind getting sucked into an abyss, where I would perform psychological self-flagellation as penance for my sin of failing to display industrious virtue. I would hoist myself out of that dark place with resolutions to change in the upcoming year. These resolutions inevitably produced disappointment by around February when old habits of procrastination and the allure of frivolities reasserted their command over me.

This holiday season I successfully avoided all masochistic meditations and found that I could acknowledge my shortcomings in a way that led to gratitude rather than self-loathing. This was made possible by reflecting on the year using one simple question: "Despite my failings this past year, what good happened?" This question revealed, even in the absence of any spectacular event, how fortunate I was this past year.

Below are some of the things I came to feel grateful for and the self-reflections on things I did this past year that led me to a deeper awareness of them:

Good fortune: I too often ate cinnamon rolls for breakfast and gorged on chocolate desserts after dinner. As for exercise, my regime consisted of little more than hastily walking to catch a city bus or running to appointments for which I was late. Did I deserve to be healthy this past year after doing so little for my health? No, yet I had the good fortune of being so.

Kindness: When my wife expressed concern to me about some neighborhood teenagers who were hanging around near our house yelling and acting wild, I dismissively said, "Don't worry about it. Just ignore them." She wanted me to listen to her and acknowledge her concern, but I did neither. Despite the fact that I was inattentive to her desire for empathy, she showed me kindness by making me dinner that evening and listening to me. I did not deserve her kindness that day, especially after neglecting her, yet despite that she was kind to me.

Tolerance: One afternoon I waited at a red light in a left-turn only lane. When the light turned green, I decided I needed to go straight. I cut off a driver coming up from behind me in the right lane who had to slam on his breaks so as not to smash into me. Rather than laying on his horn with one hand and giving me the finger with the other, which I most certainly deserved, he tolerated my carelessness and just let me go in front of him.

Forgiveness: One evening when my son, who is in middle school, did something that annoyed me on the family computer, I snapped at him saying "You idiot!" When I went to say good night to him later, I sat next to him on his bed and apologized for what I said. He looked up at me and responded, "It's okay, Dad," then patted me on the forearm. His forgiveness was a gift that engulfed me with a sense of love.

The above are only a few examples of how I came to see that failings could sometimes be tied to blessings.

As a child, when I complained to my mother about some perceived injustice done to me, she often said, "Life is not always fair." She was of course correct. Life is often unfair. But what I did not recognize for too long is that frequently I am not a victim of unfairness, but a beneficiary of it.

How did the past year go for you? Did you get all you deserved?

Thanksgiving
by Gregg Krech

For my family, the most profound part of the Thanksgiving holiday has always been a period of quiet reflection in the morning, before the commotion and chaos of the day begins. My wife, two daughters and I would each find a comfortable spot in a corner of the house. We'd pass out some paper and pencils and then sit and reflect on our blessings for about 40–45 minutes. When my daughters were toddlers and hadn't yet learned to write, we asked them to draw pictures of what they were thankful for.

Whereas Naikan uses a structure of three questions for self-reflection, here we are only using the single theme of "blessings."

It's worth taking a moment to consider the term blessing. First, it implies a favor, something which is given without having been earned. So when we think of a blessing, we think of grace. It also implies something that contributes to one's happiness or welfare. In other words, it is good fortune. And finally, there is a spiritual or holy quality to this term. For Christians, it is seen in a biblical context. Outside of Christianity, it suggests a relationship with some power beyond oneself, whatever term we may wish to call that power. So a blessing might be good fortune received which is not earned, or even deserved, and which is bestowed upon us by some power beyond oneself.

I always encourage my family to be specific in their reflections. Rather than say that "nature" is a blessing, we can say "trees." Even better, we can think of that specific maple that we use for shade in our backyard on hot summer days. Or the huge Sycamore that we love to admire on Falls Avenue. on our way to work. Specificity not only challenges our memory, but, more importantly, it deepens the experience of reflection since we are reconnecting more closely to reality, rather than just a concept.

One of the blessings that always comes up for me is the place I live. I live in a house surrounded by woods, which are, in turn, home to creatures such as owls, bobcats, coyotes, cardinals, rabbits, hawks, wild turkeys, and deer. I've lived here for 20 years. I grew up in the city and in my 20's and 30's I lived in suburbs. At that time, I dreamed of being surrounded by mountains and writing books with views of wild meadows and breaths of fresh air that would have reached me after miles of tunneling through tall pines and majestic sugar maples. I am now blessed to wake up in such a place nearly every morning.

Looking out my living room window on a weekday morning and sipping a cup of coffee, I squeeze in a moment of appreciation before I start my day. But during my Thanksgiving reflection I'm in no hurry to appreciate my life. I can wander aimlessly from blessing to blessing like a honeybee in a field of blossoms. I can allow the grace of my existence to sink into my bones where I physically experience the gift of being alive.

Sharing our reflections amongst family and friends can be a wonderful, heartwarming and intimate experience. We like to sit in the living room, with a fire going, and go through one topic at a time (like the theme of Objects or Health) as we take turns reading from the list we created. You can do this immediately after everyone finishes, or wait until evening, after dinner has ended.

Periodically, when my wife or daughter mentions one of their blessings, I'm reminded of that same blessing which I failed to consider during my own reflections. So I add it to the list – if not on paper, at least in my mind.

In the U.S., Thanksgiving occurs about five weeks before the year ends and it marks the beginning of the holiday season. As we come to the end of the year, we may feel a bit worn down by the challenges we have faced as individuals and as a family. The death of a loved one, financial problems, conflict within the family, illness, problems at work and frustration over dashed expectations may touch us in ways that leave us tired and trampled upon. We do suffer.

Reflecting on the year and our life overall helps balance our problems with the reality of how we've been cared for and the moments of joy that we experienced. It reminds us that our suffering is not the whole story. Even when our suffering feels heaviest, when it feels like it will break us – it's not the whole story. Because the whole story is much wider (in time) and much deeper (in the roots of life) and it isn't over.

Happy Thanksgiving!

Gratitude
and Gloom

"Not for everything that's given to you can you really be grateful. You can't be grateful for war in a given situation, or violence, or domestic violence, or sickness. Things like that. There are many things for which you cannot be grateful. But, in every moment, you can be grateful. For instance, the opportunity to learn something from a very difficult experience, how to grow by it, or even to protest, to stand up, and take a stand. That is a wonderful gift in a situation in which things are not the way they ought to be. So opportunity is really the key when people ask, can you be grateful for everything? No, not for everything, but in every moment."

– Brother David Steindl-Rast

Introduction:
The Loss of our Gratitude Virginity
by Gregg Krech

Most of the support we receive during the day comes from gifts or services we've received on previous occasions. Or so it seems to our mind.

We receive breakfast in bed from our partner on Sunday morning and we are surprised, pleased and grateful. The following Sunday we receive breakfast in bed again – this time delicious blueberry pancakes. We're still a bit surprised, certainly pleased and clearly grateful. Nine months later we've received breakfast in bed – blueberry pancakes, coffee, juice and an orange slice – for the 37th time. It's still nice.

It would be nicer if there were some variety – something other than pancakes. Plus, the coffee is a bit tepid. He knows I like my coffee hot. If he just poured it right before he brings it upstairs, it would certainly be hotter than this. Still, I appreciate it. I really do. Of course, I would appreciate it even more, if he would have let me sleep another half-hour.

You've lost your breakfast-in-bed virginity.

109

Do you remember when you lost your "hot water for a shower" virginity? Or your "car starts right up" virginity? Or your "contact lens" virginity? Or your "first time driving the new car" virginity? How about your "seeing the stars on a clear night" virginity?

During the brief period before we leave for work in the morning, we receive things that that we've received before: coffee maker with hot coffee, refrigerated juice, a mirror, a towel, a chair and table to sit at, a connection to the internet, our phone, water and soap to wash our dishes, clean underwear, a toothbrush. Let's add to that – oxygen to breathe, our eyesight so we can see, and, for most of us, fingers that can grab and hold objects.

There's no newness here. No surprise.

The surprise comes when there's no hot water. Or no Wi-Fi signal (stupid router!). Or our towel isn't hanging next to the shower, where it's supposed to be. So now we have to walk, dripping wet, all the way to the other side of the bathroom to get a towel. Soooooo frustrating!

We can't make ourselves feel grateful. Gratitude is more like a garden. We plant the seeds. We cultivate the soil. We keep the garden watered. We fertilize it. And it's possible, even likely, that something will sprout. And some of those sprouts won't make it – they'll be eaten by bugs or rabbits. But some of them will become full grown plants and they'll blossom into beautiful flowers.

To cultivate gratitude we notice what is done for us and given to us. We reflect on it. We express appreciation. We write thank you notes. We serve and encourage others. But we accept the fact that many of the conditions in which the garden grows are out of our control – the climate, the rain, the amount of sunlight, or an unexpected frost. An authentic experience of gratitude is more grace than it is effort. But we have to do our part (which we may also come to recognize as grace).

If we look at Naikan's three questions, we can begin to see how profound they are in cultivating gratitude. The questions do not stand alone. There is an interplay between them.

110

Question #1

"What have I received from _____?"

This question is similar to the question often posed in a gratitude journal practice where we are asked to simply make a list of what we're grateful for. However there is an important difference. If I ask myself, "What am I grateful for?" the reference point is internal. I am using my feeling state as the basis for answering this question. If the waiter brings me a tall glass of cold water and I am grateful, then the glass of water makes my list. But suppose I just had a highly charged argument with my partner. I don't feel grateful for the water. I am consumed by resentment toward my partner. So the glass of water doesn't make my list.

The phrasing of the first Naikan question points towards the objective reality of our life (usually). So at the same moment here is a partial list of what I'm receiving:

- A tall glass of water
- A menu
- A chair to sit in
- A table
- The air conditioning at the restaurant provides a cool climate on a hot day
- Electricity for the lights
- I'm able to read
- I'm able to see
- I'm not worried about paying for dinner, because I have a credit card in my wallet

The process of reflecting on my situation doesn't rely on my feeling state – it simply requires me to shift my attention so that I notice how I am being supported. Am I grateful for the items I have listed? Maybe. But to list them, in my mind or on paper, I have to notice them.

Question #2

"What have I given to _____?"

Now we turn the question around. Once again, I reflect. I have trouble thinking of something I'm giving to others at this moment. After all, I'm just sitting here by myself, waiting to order dinner. But when I walked into the restaurant, I held the door open for a couple as they were leaving. So I'll put that on my list. What else? Well, I was pleasant to the hostess when she showed me to my table. In fact, I smiled at her. I think that's something I gave. So this is my list so far:

1. Held the door for a couple leaving the restaurant.
2. Smiled at the hostess.

That's really all I can think of. Also, I'm pretty sure the hostess smiled back. Still, it's something I gave. But it's also something I received (I can add it to my first list).

Notice that my second list also doesn't require that those on the other end of my giving "feel" grateful. The assumption is that I provided something that was a benefit to the other person. Often, that is clear, but it does require some speculation. And I might be wrong. Yet the process of simply considering whether something I did provided a benefit to others is of great value to me. It allows me to practice thinking through my heart. It allows me to practice trying to understand someone else's experience. We sometimes call this empathy.

At the end of reflection on the first two questions I can see the give and take in my life for this particular time period or situation. Did I give more? Did I receive more? Not just quantity, but in value. Was it a perfectly equal exchange?

For more than 25 years I've surveyed my audiences at workshops and presentations with these exact questions. The response is overwhelmingly in favor of one of these answers? Can you guess which one?

Question #3

"What troubles and difficulties did I cause _____?"

In the restaurant example it would appear that I've really caused no trouble or difficulty. At least, not yet. Actually, when the hostess was escorting me to a table, I stopped her and asked if I could sit at a table by the window. That was a small inconvenience. But not much. I also realized that I left my cell phone in the car. So I'm not reachable by my wife and kids, or anyone, during dinner. That's only a trouble if someone is trying to reach me, and since my phone is in the car, I don't know if that's the case. I'll leave that off my list for now. When I first sat down, there were a few empty tables. Now the restaurant is full. In fact, there's at least one group waiting for a table. I'm by myself, but I'm sitting at a table that seats three. Hmmm . . . is that a trouble? What do you think?

At this point my list is rather short:

1. Inconvenienced the hostess by asking to sit at a different table.

Let's return to the theme of gratitude. When we add the second question, it may affect our experience of gratitude for the items on our first list. Remember, the first list wasn't a list of things we're grateful for – it's a list of what we've been given. As we notice those things, we may experience various levels of gratitude, or, none at all.

Gratitude simply becomes a natural response to our awareness. Someone brings me a glass of water, or makes coffee, and I notice it. My gratitude (or lack of it) is a natural response to my awareness in that moment. Remember, we are gardening. We're planting seeds and cultivating the soil. We can't control whether something grows or how quickly.

When we add in the perspective offered by the second question it gives us "context" for the first question. If I've received much more than I gave, I may find myself with a deeper appreciation of what I've been given. If I've given much more than I received, I may find myself feeling entitled, or even resentful that I didn't receive more. Keep in mind that our work is investigative. We're not trying to manipulate the answers one way or another. We're just trying to see reality clearly.

Finally, there's the third question – the troubles and difficulties I caused. What does this have to do with the cultivation of gratitude? On the surface, it has little or nothing to do with gratitude. Instead, it has everything to do with humility. This question, if we investigate it sincerely and with our defenses down, humbles us. Asking for a different table may not be particularly humbling. But as we reflect on other types of situations: forgetting to send our mom a card or gift on Mother's Day, using pirated software, having a one-night affair and never telling our partner, saying critical and demeaning things behind someone's back, stealing office supplies from work, secretly watching pornography, and the dozens, hundreds, or thousands of times we promised to have something done and were late. These items, when seen accurately and clearly and cumulatively can humble us. And even soften us.

The Anishinaabe Indians consider humility to be one of the seven great virtues. This is unusual because humility rarely shows up on a "short list" of anybody's virtues. Mark Thompson, a contemporary member of the Anishinaabe, provides a concise but poignant explanation of the meaning of humility when he says,

"When we learn humility, we learn to put ourselves where we belong in this universe."

When we are truly humbled, we are more likely to feel naturally grateful. In fact, genuine humility can allow us to go beyond gratitude to grace. Grace is not just appreciating what we are given. It's the recognition that we didn't earn what we've been given. We may not even deserve what we've been given. We are blessed, in various ways, not because of how we have lived – how we have conducted ourselves in relationships over the years. We are blessed in spite of it.

Victor Hugo, says it most eloquently:

"The supreme happiness of life
is the conviction that we are loved -
Loved for ourselves, or rather,
Loved in spite of ourselves."

Gratitude: The Antidote to Gloom in Rough Times
by Kurt Barstow

I have not been going through the easiest of times lately. In recent months, I've had to go on food stamps, as I am seeking employment. This new dependency started out as an occasion of dread and humiliation – an opportunity to reflect on life's disappointments and my failures.

Looked at through the lens of gratefulness, however, it became something to receive with great thanks as I consider the taxpayers I will never know who contributed to my sustenance, the massive bureaucracy and workers that keep the food stamp program running, and the politicians who passed legislation for this kind of thing in the first place. Besides that, of course, there is everything else involved in eating—the earth, the sun, the rain, the animals and vegetables that give their lives, the farmers, the factory workers, the truckers, the grocery stores, and the check-out person. All this and more is behind a simple meal that I prepare.

And this is not even to mention, in terms of my current economic condition, the assistance I have received from family and friends. From the point of view of gratitude, no matter what my passing feelings about my circumstances might be, I am always living in abundance, and I am always living a life that is interconnected to everything else. It might be said that gratitude is the awareness of that interconnectedness and of the universe's extraordinary ability to consistently provide.

Naikan has been a very helpful resource. Naikan means "looking inside." It is a simple process of self-reflection that was invented in the 1940s by Ishin Yoshimoto. The heart of Naikan is to be found in three questions:

- What have I received from _____?
- What have I given to _____?
- What troubles and difficulties have I caused _____?

These questions can be posed about people, groups, institutions, life-forms, body parts, inanimate objects, or a period of time, among other things. Rather than deriving from mere sentimentalism or false humility, Naikan is a reality-based practice. It gets one out of one's head and emotions and into what really happened. Gregg Krech, author of Naikan: Gratitude, Grace and the Japanese Art of Self-Reflection, reflects on his wife in a very concrete way:

"My wife made me fresh-squeezed orange juice this morning. She washed my breakfast dishes. She gave me the watch I'm wearing. These are all simple, clear descriptions of reality. Her attitude or motivation does not change the fact that I benefited from her effort. Often we take such things for granted. We hurry through our day giving little attention to all the 'little' things we are receiving. But are these things really little? They only seem so because, while we are being supported, our attention is elsewhere. But when there is no hot water for a shower or we lose our glasses, these little things grab our attention."

Furthermore, when something really big goes wrong we forget the vast majority of things that are going right. The battery in my car may have died, but the rent was paid, all my internal organs are working perfectly and there is food for dinner. To see only the dead battery is actually unrealistic. By means of a thorough and regular reflection on what we are given, however, our attention broadens to the larger reality we are living.

In the second question, we are asked what we have given. It almost always seems the case that this list ends up being disappointingly short compared to what we have received. This only makes sense since we are but one individual and there is a whole world out there that conspires for our benefit and that includes other people, nature, technology, commerce, and thousands of years of culture.

Even if you're doing something as altruistic as heading up The Clinton Global Initiative, it's hard to compete with the sun, oxygen, gravity, water, the Internet, all the engineering and construction that goes into making a city, airline travel, the collections of business people and government officials that collaborate on projects, all the people that work for your institution, and the ideas and theories that made any of it possible in the first place. The point is, for all of us, that in the ledger of what the world owes us and what we owe the world, it is likely to be we who are in debt to the world. Again, this is just realism.

Krech says, *"As we reflect on our life we begin to see the reality of our life. We may find ourselves asking: What is more appropriate - to go through life with the mission of collecting what is owed us, or to go through life trying to repay our debt to others?"*

The third question involves even more soul searching. To reflect regularly on the problems we have caused others involves another shift of attention. We are usually preoccupied with the wrongs that have been done to us, so much so that we don't give much thought to the difficulties we cause others. My unemployment, for example, has put tremendous pressures on my partner, family members, and friends, who have helped out with money.

With this question, we are forced to move beyond a victim mentality or justifications about our life and actions in order to take care of our own side of the street. This question is particularly important because of our propensity to judge others and our natural inclination to want to preserve a virtuous self-image. In order to change behavior, however, we must first see the reality, tarnished as it might be.

In our current world, where harsh − even violent − divisiveness is often the rule and so many people are still intolerant of others who might deviate from their narrowly-prescribed beliefs, perhaps gratitude can provide a common link through which we can soften some of our rougher edges. As a widespread practice it would certainly have implications for all our relationships, including the one most threatened right now − our relationship to the earth.

If we want to lead a richer, more positive, less self-obsessed, less conflict-ridden, more environmentally sound, more loving life, the personal practice of cultivating an authentic sense of gratitude seems a good place to start.

Grateful for Nothing

by Gregg Krech

My friend Donna had an interesting experience a while ago—she compared it to winning the lottery. She was so touched by this experience that she mentioned how grateful she was for things she normally takes for granted every day: water, trees, electricity and more. So what kind of extraordinary good fortune came Donna's way? Why was she feeling so grateful, so lucky? Here's what happened: Nothing happened.

You see, Donna lives near Vero Beach, Florida, and a hurricane was heading in her direction. She and her husband did everything they could to prepare for the storm – for 90 mph winds and drenching rains. But nothing happened. A few gusts of wind – some intermittent rain. That was it. That's why Donna felt like she won the lottery. Nothing happened.

When was the last time you felt grateful because nothing happened? Nobody crashed into your car on the way home from work. The electricity didn't go out. You didn't wake up with a toothache. You didn't have a heart attack. Nobody shot at you or robbed your home while you were gone.

There are people who are living in war zones at this very moment. Just look at the news and you can find those areas on a map. Many of those people are very aware at the end of the day that nobody in their family was killed and their home wasn't destroyed by a bomb or hand grenade. Because they live with that awareness every day, they also are aware when nothing happens to hurt them.

And yet when you expect to die or you expect your home to be destroyed, "nothing happened" is like winning the lottery.

If you're reading this, there's a good chance your life is relatively safe—so safe that you spend most days without thinking about the issue of safety. You're so safe that safety isn't on your mind. So when nothing happens, you don't feel particularly grateful. You expect to be safe, just as you expect the light to go on when you hit the switch on the wall.

118

My friend Donna, described her experience . . .

"The extraordinary thing about this hurricane is that everyone knew it was coming. For days, the weather channels tracked the hurricane moving up the eastern seaboard and predicting where it would turn west and hit land. Generally we don't get much advance warning with natural disasters like earthquakes or tornados. So tens of millions of people watched and waited. And the force of the hurricane destroyed homes, turned cars into boats, and, in some cases, took lives. But for millions of people, "nothing happened." We sat safely in our homes and watched the gusts of wind and listened to the rain on our roofs while we read a book and checked our email. And many of us experienced a sincere and authentic moment of gratefulness. We were worried, anxious, even fearful. And nothing happened."

So here's our challenge: to allow our hearts and minds to be touched by gratitude without the presence of a hurricane. To appreciate life and the grace by which we wake up each day and go to sleep in safety. To recognize that our personal safety is a gift and something we have little control over. We may survive a hurricane and have a heart attack the next day. Our lives are all hanging by a thread. It makes us nervous to think about it, so we try not to. But that thread has held us up since we were born. And once in a while it's good to notice it so we can be thankful for it.

"Nothing happened" isn't particularly exciting. It's not as entertaining as a good movie. It's not intellectually challenging, nor is it adorable like a baby kitten. And yet when you expect to die or you expect your home to be destroyed, "nothing happened" is like winning the lottery. It's worthy of celebration. A celebration of the fact that despite all of our problems and aches and pains and financial challenges and relationship conflicts we're alive and we're breathing and at the moment, we're safe. So take a moment and sit back. And breathe in "nothing happened." And breathe out a breath of thanks. Gratitude for just being able to breathe. Now that's really something!

The Luckiest Man on the Face of the Earth

by Lou Gehrig

*You may have heard of Lou Gehrig, the famous baseball player who played for the New York Yankees in the 1930's. Gehring had been diagnosed with ALS, (aka Lou Gehrig's Disease), and was forced to retire from baseball. He played in over 2,300 consecutive games, a record which stood for 56 years, giving him the name **Lou Gehrig - Iron Horse**. What follows is an excerpt from the speech he gave at his last game. The speech was given to a capacity crowd at Yankee Stadium.*

"Fans, for the past two weeks you have been reading about the bad break I got. Yet today I consider myself the luckiest man on the face of this earth. I have been in ballparks for seventeen years and have never received anything but kindness and encouragement from you fans.

Look at these grand men. Which of you wouldn't consider it the highlight of his career just to associate with them for even one day? Sure I'm lucky. Who wouldn't consider it an honor to have known Jacob Ruppert? Also, the builder of baseball's greatest empire, Ed Barrow?

To have spent six years with that wonderful little fellow, Miller Huggins? Then to have spent the next nine years with that outstanding leader, that smart student of psychology, the best manager in baseball today, Joe McCarthy?

Sure I'm lucky. When the New York Giants, a team you would give your right arm to beat, and vice versa, sends you a gift – that's something. When everybody down to the groundskeepers and those boys in white coats remember you with trophies – that's something. When you have a wonderful mother-in-law who takes sides with you in squabbles with her own daughter – that's something.

When you have a father and a mother who work all their lives so you can have an education and build your body – it's a blessing. When you have a wife who has been a tower of strength and shown more courage than you dreamed existed – that's the finest I know.

So I close in saying that I may have had a tough break, but I have an awful lot to live for."

– Lou Gehrig, July 4, 1939

The Objects
of our
Attention

> *"One of the characteristics of man which distinguishes him from the animals is that he has acquired the custom of wearing clothes. You and I have worn an infinite number of various kinds of clothing since we were born. They have been the products of the labor, imagination, and skill of countless, unknown people and they have been purchased by the sacrifices of our families and ourselves. A garment is not just a piece of cloth that is lifeless, because the vast interrelationship of men and the hidden workings of nature are contained within a single, unpretentious garment."*
>
> – Rev. Gyodo Haguri

Introduction
by Gregg Krech

Some of us are on the path of accumulation. We are accumulating more objects and we hope to experience the benefits or pleasure those objects can offer us. Some of us are on the path of reduction. We are trying to minimize the objects we possess. We want a life with less clutter, less repair, less maintenance. Then there are those who have the idea of reducing our possessions, but, in reality, continue to accumulate more of them. Very few of us are engaged in the practice of noticing and appreciating the objects in our life. It is a path worthy of our attention.

We are mostly reminded of the value of an object when it is broken, when it is no longer functioning, when it ceases to serve us. Actually, it's not that we are reminded to appreciate the object. Rather, when something is no longer working, we notice our own inconvenience. We express frustration, feel disappointed, even get angry.

When we take charge of a new object, we expect that it will provide undiminished service to us whenever we need it. We press a button, and we receive hot coffee. We press another button, and we receive music. We turn a key (or press a button) and the car starts and the engine purrs. I still possess a few non-electronic

125

objects, but have the same expectations: The middle-C on the piano will produce a perfectly tuned note when pressed by my index finger. The wood stove will heat up, warm up the living room and release smoke through the chimney. The silver faucet handle on the kitchen sink will offer water when turned to the left, and contain the water when turned to the right.

Yet even those of us who are trying to simplify our lives depend on objects for our comfort and existence. Objects are instruments of our care.

Think about your experience this morning. What objects were involved in caring for you? Coffee machine, cup, refrigerator, furnace, walls, roof, electrical outlet, cell phone, computer, wifi router, car, sink, clothing, shoes, stove, eyeglasses, contact lenses, watch, stop signs, car radio, sofa, chair, desk, hairbrush.

Consider the karmic ingredients of each of these items. They were created from raw material, machinery, human hands, and human minds that designed them. They were kept in warehouses and transported by delivery vehicles and drivers. A large network of people, objects and energy made it possible for you to brush your hair this morning. Another completely different network of people made it possible to see what you were doing (if you used a mirror). The objects that serve us may not be alive, but they contain the energy of many lives. And they are couriers of care, support, even joy.

I can recall several occasions when an object has saved my life. Most recently, it was my bicycle helmet, which protected my head when I flipped over the handlebars and landed on a concrete road. A seat belt probably saved my life in a collision I had on an icy Illinois road about 35 years ago. Living in Vermont, a good pair of gloves and thermal socks have protected my fingers and toes from frostbite. Snow tires have allowed me to drive safely on icy, snow-covered roads. A little blue book called a passport has allowed me to travel freely around the world. And locks on doors have kept me safe when I traveled to places where dangers might pose a risk.

Reflecting on objects using Naikan's three questions is a curious process because we often find that while we are served by objects, we give little in return. The care we do provide (like automobile maintenance) is done simply so we can get more and better service from those objects.

When we reflect on the service provided by an object, we honor that object – we honor the lives that were given so that object could exist.

We think of ourselves as owners of an object because we have exchanged money to acquire it. But it may be more realistic, and compassionate, to think of ourselves as stewards. These objects are placed in our care and we have a responsibility to carry out our responsibilities just as they do. When we look around the room, we should realize that some of these objects may outlive us. At some point our bodies will be disposed of just as we disposed of that old toaster oven.

The existence of human lives and object lives are time-limited. During the time we are given, we care for one another. We provide care and we receive it. And to notice that, consistently, enriches our own experience.

Walls Separate Us, but They Also Connect Us

by Les MacFarlane

T he process of reflecting on our lives known as Naikan can help us see the miracles of life and reveal how connected we are to one another. The more we immerse ourselves in such reflection, the more new paths and questions arise that reveal the intricate web of interdependence we all share.

While one of my students was telling me about her Naikan reflection, she mentioned that she had received shelter from the walls of her home. It was an excellent point and one that I had seldom considered. Walls, however, are a big part of our lives, or at least my life. Recently, I had the opportunity to build some walls with my father-in-law and saw the immense effort and sacrifice that goes into keeping people warm, dry and comfortable. Here are some things I learned about walls.

"I'm learning from my father-in-law, but who taught him how to build walls?"

In order to get started, it is essential to obtain supplies and that's relatively easy thanks to countless beings. It is quite remarkable to think that in the past, people used to cut down trees, cut logs for the home and build their homes without electricity or the convenience of a hardware or lumber store. It's a blessing to be able to drive a couple of minutes and pick up wood and almost any necessarily supplies.

"What was involved in making the vehicle and building roads to drive to the hardware and lumber stores?"

"What does it take to get a full-grown tree to a mill many miles away? If you needed to do this yourself, what would you do?"

While there are now steel studs for construction most people still use two-by-fours for framing their walls and they're one of the first supplies to be purchased. When

128

we arrive at the lumber yard the wood has been forested from trees that sacrifice their lives. Once the trees get to the mill, they are cut into two-by-fours. However, that's not the end of the process because the two-by-fours are then dressed. Dressing is a process that involves planing the faces and edges of the two-by-four so it's the proper thickness and looks smooth. This results in two-by-fours actually being 3.2" by 1.2". The wood is then loaded, transported, unloaded and sold – a process that involves hundreds of people. This amazing amount of effort is simply the work that goes into the two-by-fours. There is little doubt that the processes for the nails, sheathing materials, drywall, drywall screws, drills, hammers, levels, carpenter squares, the various saws and other elements used in building a wall, are equally complicated and important.

Once the supplies are at the house, a frame needs to be built. The frame is the skeleton of the wall. It is constructed in sections – one wall at a time. The pieces are nailed together ensuring that the studs are exactly 16 or 24 inches away from each other, on center. That means that the middle of one stud is 16 inches from the center of the next stud. This makes sheathing easier and gives a strong wall. This process requires attention. The distances must be marked accurately and the studs must be nailed in the proper place. For most of us, someone we don't even know paid attention to this to ensure that our house is strong and set to standard measurements so that we are safe.

Once the electrical, plumbing, and insulation work is done in the wall, drywall is installed. Drywall is a large sheet (often 4' x 8') of gypsum. It is heavy and requires strength and skill to put up. I have never met anyone, except a professional, who enjoys putting up drywall.

Once the sheets of drywall are cut to size and attached to the frame, the seams need to be covered with tape and a drywall compound known as "mud". The mud is allowed to dry and is then sanded to create the wall's flat, smooth appearance. There is little doubt in my mind that the people who do this "mudding, taping and sanding" are true artists. Professional drywallers use just the right amount of mud so that there is little sanding to do. The drywallers are subject to inhaling a great deal of dust and often wear masks because it is unhealthy to inhale the dust. In essence, this means that someone has risked his or her health in order for us to have walls.

Walls are then papered or painted, trimmed and generally finished. When most of us walk into a home, the walls are seamless and the work and skill is invisible. They can become just the background. But these walls are the result of hours of training, practice and sacrifice. It is like the Zen saying "When the shoe fits, we forget about the shoe".

As I write this piece early morning in November, I occasionally look out my window. There is snow and ice on the ground, yet I sit here in a t-shirt as I write. The walls of this house, made by someone I don't know, are what separate me from the cold. Thanks to these walls for keeping me dry and warm. Thanks to the framers, insulators, drywallers, drivers and sales people. While it may seem strange to thank the walls and the people who built them, when it comes down to it, the difference between having a home and being homeless is walls.

Musings on the Kindness of Objects Inspired by Naikan

by Anne-Carine Oskarsen

In November 2009, I enrolled as an eager participant in the ToDo Institute's Month of Self Reflection distance learning course. I started off strong, supported by inspiring articles, valuable comments in the discussion forum and alluring daily tasks. But, somewhere along the way, resistance started to develop. It became tough to sit down quietly and reflect in silence. Things started coming up that I wasn't proud of—hidden sides of myself that were unpleasant to encounter.

The more it became obvious that I owe the world, the greater my resistance. I tried the intellectual way of dealing with the course exercises, but it became forced. I started developing an attitude of wanting to "graduate" from gratitude as soon as possible. Just get my diploma—"been there, done that." I quit halfway through the course.

But something had started stirring. I was looking at things in a different way. I was reading about Buddhism and the mind-heart of everything, including inanimate objects. I began writing small texts every now and then. Eventually, I created my own small-scale project of self-reflection. It may be grand to recognize how much my mother has done for me, but right now it feels profound to ponder the fact that my cell phone is pretty useful in my daily life, even though I treat it like trash.

Starting to work with your attention is like peeling an onion. You realize something and the outer layer of the onion falls off, only to reveal the second layer within … and then the third and the fourth. But once you've started, it's hard to stop, especially when you start thinking about the creamy, lovely onion soup you will enjoy in the end!

131

Shoes

I step on you
every day.
I brutally pull you away from your quiet sleep in the
hall. facing mud. facing dog shit (sorry), the unbearable
stickiness of chewing gum.
you go wherever I go, voluntarily or not.
have I ever thanked you? hardly.
my attention rather goes to the fact that you are not
brand new, not the latest fashion, be even worthy of
consideration.
yet you
protect the fragileness of my feet. I can face the world
with you, still dry and warm despite returning rain.
I can run for the bus that I simply cannot miss. explore
my surroundings, still comfortable and cool.

Doors

thanks to you
privacy, seclusion
a moment of peaceful reflection in solitude
you give me the chance to step in and step out,
to open and close - at my will!
if there were no doors, I think the general
draft in the world might get too big.
there is such comfort in closing a door
sometimes, just as there can be immense
pleasure in opening one.

Eyeglasses

without you
I am helpless.
as simple as that.

Cellphone

with you I am always connected.
my loved ones are nothing but a button push away.
you give me protection, help and guidance within
easy reach wherever I am.
the possibilities you render. hearing the crystal clear
voice of someone a thousand miles away. yet…
you're pretty small. getting increasingly scratched,
suffering countless falls to the ground.
the extent to which I depend on you is hardly
reflected in how you're being treated.
you remain a blessing and a curse. perhaps I
emphasize the latter. perhaps you deserve to be
regarded more often as the first.

Backpack

I put you everywhere.
I throw you on the ground.
you slip through my fingers and I let you fall.
yet
you carry all what is precious to me without
complaining.
I don't take care of you, I often wish you
looked different. still you tirelessly perform

your obligations, always willing, as long as I
can remember where I last put you down.

Church bell

dividing the day into manageable blocks
of 30 minutes
letting every citizen of the town know
through your penetrating sound that
life is ticking
moment by moment
running out of our hands like sand

Tatami mat

you support me, though I often complain about
your hardness.
thank you for showing me how my physical body
still maintains blockages and tenseness preventing
my blood from flowing as I sleep.
I can rest knowing what is underneath me is pure,
natural, steady and won't move an inch.
thank you, tatami, for your heaviness.
even though my mind might sail on many oceans
in my dreams, my body won't float away on
something so heavily connected to the ground.
when I clean my room, moving you around helps
me develop stamina and strength. I think I
should move you more often, rather than letting
you collect as much dust as you do.

Barefoot and Grateful

by Rami Shapiro

What are you grateful for?

Start with the biggies: your kids, your marriage (maybe your divorce), life, a good job (or maybe just a job), family, friends, that kind of stuff. Then work on the Hallmark things: babies, puppies, daisies, sunsets, and babies playing with puppies among the daisies at sunset.

But what about your shoes? Are you grateful for your shoes?

Before you answer this question, take a close look at your shoes. You may have more than one pair, so pick the pair you wear the most. If they are in your closet, go and examine them. If they are on your feet, take them off, and let's have a look.

Start with the soles. Are they worn down or have you had your shoes resoled recently? What about the backs of the shoes: are they crushed from cramming your feet into the shoes by forcing the backs down to make room for the ball of your foot? When you take your shoes off, do you untie them or just crush the backs with the ball of the opposite foot and kick them off? Even if they are loafers, do you take them off or scrape them off? And when you do take them off, where do you put your shoes? Do you toss them in a closet where they can be stepped on as you rummage for other things, or do you fill them out with a shoetree? How shiny are your shoes? When was the last time you polished them? Are your shoelaces in good condition or are they frayed and about to wear through?

Keep the answers in mind as you walk about outside barefoot. Go ahead – walk about a block without your shoes on to protect your feet. Some people live in areas where walking barefoot is hazardous. Even those who don't, usually find walking without shoes painful when rocks, sticks, and debris tear into their feet.

So let me ask you again: *Are you grateful for your shoes?*

Of course you are. They protect your feet, and your feet need protecting. And even if your feet need no protection, there are some restaurants you love visiting that won't let you in without shoes. So, if for no other reason, you may feel grateful to your shoes because they get you into those restaurants to eat. But feeling grateful isn't enough. Do you show gratitude to your shoes? Does your feeling grateful translate into being grateful, and does your being grateful translate into your doing grateful?

The answer is in your shoes. Broken back shoes, scuffed shoes, worn down shoes, shoes that show signs of neglect and abuse answer the question about gratitude far more powerfully than any words you might utter or emotions you might feel. Gratitude is more than something you feel, it is something you do. Gratitude is a verb.

I own five pairs of shoes. I have a pair of running shoes, a pair of loafers, a pair of dress shoes, and two pairs of Crocs, one for wearing in the house and one for wearing outside. My dress shoes are made by Rockport. They look like wingtips on the outside and feel like running shoes on the inside.

These particular shoes have to be sent to the manufacturer to be resoled. The first time I did this, the shoes were returned to me in near mint condition accompanied by a handwritten letter signed by the person who did the repair. I assumed this was a preprinted form letter, but that assumption proved false as I read the brief note:

Dear Rabbi Shapiro,

We at Rockport take great pride in the quality of our work and our product. It is clear to me from the condition of your shoes, however, that you do not. The backs are cracked from improper use; the leather is dry from insufficient cleaning and polishing; and the overall look of the shoe is sloppy. On behalf of all of us who work hard to offer you a quality product, I wish you would take better care of our shoes.

In the box along with the shoes and the note was a shoe cleaning kit complete with polish and a brush.

These people were serious about their work and wanted me to treat their shoes as if they were my own. Wait a minute – they are my own! These are the shoes that protect my feet from all kinds of dangers: hot sidewalks, jagged rocks, broken glass, discarded hypodermic needles, human vomit, duck droppings, and dog poop — I walk in some pretty rough places — so why don't I live the gratitude I say I feel toward my shoes? Because I treat them as an It, an object to be exploited, rather than a Thou, a presence to be honored.

As it turned out, what was true about my shoes was true about my toothbrush, the plumbing in my home, and even the plumbing in my body. In turned out to be true about most of the things in my life, and perhaps the people as well.

Most of you are probably aware of this and do your best to cultivate I–Thou connections rather than I–It ones. But let me share a practice with you that you may not know. It is a Jewish practice called *Asher Yatzar*, "Who forms humanity." Whenever you go to the bathroom and move your bowels or empty your bladder, recite this prayer. I have it printed out and framed where I can see it while I'm sitting on the toilet. Here is my rendition of the Hebrew.

Blessed are You, Yah, Source and Substance of all creation, Who gives rise to me as an ocean gives rise to waves. My body is a marvel of openings and closings, fills and hollows. If that which should close, not close; or that which should open, not open, I could not survive. Yet over these I have no control. I owe my very being to their proper functioning, and I am made humble and grateful with this knowing. Blessed are You, Yah, Who opens and closes, rises and falls, all in the wondrous dance of being and becoming.

The seeds of gratitude are found in the strangest places, aren't they?

To 0078 with Love

by Victoria Register-Freeman

Where is it written the Average Jane can't benefit from the services of a personal shopper? Why are these helpful individuals inevitably seen as the sole property of persons like Roma, Christie, and Demi? At the financial low point of my life – a time when I was recently divorced and had to divide monthly bills into three piles: must pay, might pay, can't pay – I too, acquired a personal shopper. Just like the media glitterati, I had someone who shopped and inevitably purchased clothes that were the perfect fit and the perfect color for me.

I discovered my personal shopper one Friday afternoon when I had to purchase a suit for a second job. My first job was teaching seventh grade English, and it was a job I truly loved. However, it was also a job that didn't pay enough to keep a teenager in braces and soccer cleats.

Therefore, when I was offered a chance to pay off my rotund credit card balance by presenting weekend teacher recertification seminars, I accepted the offer gladly. Unfortunately, the recertification job required a serious suit, and most of my suits weren't serious enough. Quite a few of them sported red ink stains from paper grading and the others featured sprung rumps from lunchroom duty.

Muttering the adage, "Beware of all enterprises that require new clothes," I trudged into a neighborhood consignment shop hoping to outfit myself on the thirty dollars I had saved by switching long distance carriers. There, to my amazement, I found an Anne Klein suit that fit perfectly along with a pair of sleek black slacks. These items provided me with two highly professional looking outfits for $27.32 – an amount that left room for new pantyhose.

When I paid for the items at the counter, I noticed that the saleswoman credited both of them to 0078. "What's that?" I asked. "Oh, that's the number of the consignee," she answered. "People who consign regularly get an ongoing account number. 0078 has a very active account."

And that's how I acquired my very own personal shopper, 0078, who stylishly outfitted me for years. Like the original James Bond whose signature number she almost bears, 0078 has impeccable taste in clothing. She likes tailored suits with mid-calf skirts and hip-length, fitted jackets. She prefers jewel necklines and the colors scarlet and black and cobalt, colors I've loved since my paper doll days.

There are a few other things I have learned about her. First, she has a well-developed social side. Despite her serious suits, 0078 must, as my teenage sons say, "party hard". At the close of each season she consigns a few cocktail dresses, usually Princess Di affairs with strapless tops and plunging necklines. Second, she is a woman who leaves no marks on her attire. Like the mythical Marine Corps drill sergeants at Paris Island, she appears not to sweat, nor have I ever found any sign of actual human habitation on anything she has consigned: no sprung rumps, coffee stains, baby burp marks or ash burns and definitely no pen marks or chalk dust – two touches I usually take it upon myself to add.

Living in a relatively large southern city, I may never meet 0078, but I occasionally fantasize that such a meeting may take place. At that moment I would tell her how much she had added to my life. Having her as my personal shopper has enabled me not only to out-dress my budget, but also to spend less time pawing through sale items and more time curled up with Keats. In addition, her clothing has added adventure to my bookish life. I imagine the locales where she has worn these same suits to break hearts, make deals, do lunch, and catch 747s to New York for off-Broadway openings.

Most importantly, I want to thank her for moving up a size in sync with my own expansion. We both moved from size ten to size twelve at the same time. Of course, my pounds came from cheese grits in the school cafeteria. I like to think hers came from caviar in Cannes.

Wake Up – You Have a Body

Whether or not the glass is half empty or half full –
you still have a glass.
And that's something.
And how do you know you have a glass?
You can see it and feel it – you have sensory experience.
Which means you're alive and that's a miracle.
So whether the glass is half-empty or half-full . . . it's a miracle!

– Gregg Krech

Introduction:
How to Wake Up!

By Gregg Krech

Have you ever had this experience? Your alarm goes off and you find yourself lying in bed as your mind and body begin to awake to the morning. Your mind quickly gets into gear like a computer booting up when you hit the "power" button. Thoughts begin to arise. You begin thinking about the day, about everything you have to do today. Meetings, deadlines, phone calls that need to be made. You begin anticipating the overwhelming demands that life will place on you today. Periodically, your mind slips in a wild card, like, "I should have gone to bed earlier," or, "Why did I waste my time watching that stupid TV show last night?" You think about your schedule. Your to-do list begins to take form like a genie mysteriously emerging from a bottle, but instead of granting you a wish, it's reminding you of how much you need to do today.

When you finally emerge from your warm bed and your bare feet make contact with the floor, you've created some fuel for getting the day started. But what kind of fuel is it? It's the fuel of anxiety, of stress over how much there is to do. It's the

143

fuel of depression about how impossible this life is and how challenging the coming day is likely to be. It's the fuel of self-absorption and anticipation—the fuel of fear that you won't be able to handle what life will place in your path today.

Is this the fuel you want to use to get yourself going this morning?

An alternative is to use those first few moments of awareness mindfully, in a way that anchors you right in the present moment of your life. I discovered this after spending too many mornings going through the script I described above. Then one morning I realized that everything that was going on in my mind had nothing to do with the present moment of my life. So I lay in bed and simply tried to notice the truth of my life and found that I was not only more mindful, but the experience naturally stimulated a sense of gratitude and appreciation. This practice became a marriage between mindfulness and Naikan, a method of self-reflection which originated in Japan.

Here's an example of the flow of my attention as I practice this "first awareness of the morning":

I'm lying next to my beautiful, sleeping wife and enjoying the warmth emanating from her body. The temperature outside is chilly, but I'm kept warm by this cozy, thick blanket and the furnace and fuel in the basement of this house.

My two sweet daughters, the blessings of my life, are sleeping quietly in the next room.

My sweet dog, Barley, our family's golden retriever, is sleeping quietly on his little futon next to my bed. I reach over the bed and caress his soft coat. I feel the quality of this softness against my fingers, the first awareness I have of my sense of touch today.

I wiggle my toes and they all work fine. I stretch and jiggle my fingers and they all work fine.

I am safe, and my safety has been preserved throughout the night even though I slept and had no awareness of my surroundings.

My eyes have now adjusted to the dim light. I can still see. I am able to begin the day by seeing the extraordinary colors and shapes of the room that surround me.

I take a deep breath and my lungs fill themselves with air. My body has been doing this for me all night without my conscious help and now, for a moment, I take the lead and bring my attention to this amazing process of breathing which sustains my body and spirit.

I listen. For a moment there is complete silence. I listen to the silence. What a gift that silence is. Then I hear a sound: a bird, perhaps a crow. Now more crow sounds. I can hear. There is life outside my home. The world is waking up. I can hear the world waking up. What a gift it is to hear the sounds of the world.

I squeeze my pillow against my cheek. I'm tempted to stay here longer in this warm, cozy little cocoon. It takes a moment of will, a moment of determination to abandon this warmth and safety and venture into the world.

My mind is yearning to make its to-do list—to remind me of all the details, tasks and work that awaits me. I will make that list soon. But not now.

First I have to feel the texture of the firm carpet against the soles of my feet as my body emerges stiffly, awkwardly, imperfectly into verticality, and I am blessed with the beginning of a new day.

Thanks to My Body: Reflections on Turning 70
by Margaret McKenzie

On a chilly, gray day near the end of October, I celebrated my 70th birthday. I asked family and friends to join me in a nearby forest preserve where we staged a reenactment of my 10th birthday party. Hot dogs and chips were the order of the day. The grand finale, rather than a cake, was "s'mores" – a favorite treat from my Girl Scout days. This forest preserve also featured a sledding hill. When two of my grandchildren decided to roll down the hill, three of my fellow crones and I joined them. What a remarkable feeling – the pull of gravity speeding us down the hill, our usually carefully-defended hips and shoulders thumping against the ground. We arrived at the bottom laughing like 10-year-olds and praising our bones for not breaking.

A few days later, though, I was no longer laughing. Upon waking, I discovered my wrists, knee and shoulder, which are subject to minor arthritis, were aching. I hadn't slept well and felt mentally foggy. Worst of all, the previous day I had made two appointments for surgery – one dental, the second with my gynecologist. "What is wrong with you?" I complained to my body. "Why are you having these problems?" I lay there in bed, counting my aches and pains and then (thankfully) another thought crept in. "You know, you are 70 years old," I told myself. "Even though you have these problems, many of your parts and functions are working just fine." Maybe it was time to examine the facts more closely. I decided to use the helpful tool of Naikan reflection to assess the state of my body more realistically. This is what I found.

What has my body given to me?

1. My feet helped me stand up 69 years ago, and they have been walking me everywhere ever since. They have carried me up and down mountain paths, regularly taken me on daily walks of a mile or more. If my pedometer is to be trusted, on most days they transport me about 7500 steps through my work and

leisure life.

2. My legs have accompanied my feet on all these many miles and additionally have the neat trick of bending at the knee – making it possible for me to get into cupboards, look under the bed, and get eye to eye with my grandchildren when they were babies. My knees make it possible for me to sit in chairs and stand up. As a young woman, my legs allowed me to swim a mile a day, ride a bike, and run down the street. My wonderful knees endured being folded and immovable as I sat through 10 years of Zen meditation.

3. Of course, where would my legs and feet be if it were not for my hips? At age 70, my hips remain flexible and trustworthy – bending me in and out of cars and making bicycle riding possible. And a special thanks to them for the years they supported my babies with no complaint whatsoever.

4. When I get to the "body" part of my body – the oval container that holds the organs that keep me running everyday – it becomes harder to tally up the number of services and functions my body provides. It would take quite some time to describe all the chemical processes that support my life. For example, my digestive system has processed, distributed and disposed of 78,000 meals. At an estimate of one pound per meal, that would be about 34 tons of food. And that does not factor in the bagels, ice cream cones, and chocolate chip cookies that were added to the meal. And my heart – what stamina! Forty two million beats per lifetime? No . . . per year! Thank you so much heart, lungs, stomach and their friends for working so efficiently and continuously. All without any thought or effort from me. Arms, elbows, hands, fingers – the famous opposable thumbs; sometimes a little stiff – but working wonderfully. Opening jars, carrying 25-pound bags of salt, knitting small hats and, of course, writing these words.

5. And then there is my head – eyes, ears, nose, mouth, and teeth. Some of these parts have needed some extra upkeep, but thanks to my dentist and optometrist they're as good as new. Busy chewing kale, tasting Chai tea, smelling the grass just after the rain, hearing my kitty Gracie's purr and best of all looking at the sun,

147

moon, grass, books and my family's faces. And hair! My hair is still all there!

6. Skin still covering all of me – sagging a little here and there but doing a great job of keeping me contained – preventing my insides from spilling onto sidewalks and carpets.

7. Last and best, my brain. I think it's doing okay. A little slow at times, a little foggy, but still able to balance my checkbook and remember the words to "You Are My Sunshine".

What have I given my body?

1. Most of my life, I've given my body good food. For the past seven years I've been on a vegan diet. My body responded by – under its own direction – recovering from a serious autoimmune disorder.

2. I give my body a couple of quarts of water most days.

3. I take my body walking – about 7500 steps a day.

4. I take my body to an exercise class once a week.

5. About 30 years ago, I relieved my body of the job of dealing with alcohol and tobacco.

6. I send my body to bed each night and leave it there for seven hours of rest.

7. I give my body a hot shower most days, which it likes quite a lot.

What trouble have I caused my body?

1. When my body was younger, I was abusive to it. I drank excessively and smoked a great deal. During this time my body was very unhappy, often feeling ill and getting sick.

2. For 10 years, I caused my body to carry an extra 15 pounds of fat.

3. As a young adult, I neglected appropriate dental care resulting in a lot of trouble for my teeth as I aged.

4. I periodically refused to ask for help in moving heavy objects and injured my back muscles as a result .

5. I don't stretch the muscles of my body as frequently as I should, causing them to contract and stiffen.
6. Sometimes I give my body more food than it can accommodate, giving it a stuffed and uncomfortable feeling.
7. My feet have asked for new shoes, yet I continue to ignore their request.

Making this brief assessment of the state of the body helped me get a perspective on my current situation. Much as I'd like to put my body in a time machine and return to age 15 (not my brain, you'll note), that's not going to happen. I am very fortunate to have reached this age with so many systems in good shape. I have outlived my parents and my grandparents. I now am heading for my great grandfather, who would reminisce about his days sailing large full-sailed boats on the Great Lakes when he was 94.

In the course of writing this essay, I noticed my tendency to moan when I get out of the shower. I would be bending around, drying various limbs, as I moaned and complained. I decided that, although I can't change the state of my body, I could choose my response to that state. So now in the morning, instead of moaning and groaning, I say "Wheeeeee!! Wheeeeeee!!". It always makes me laugh. Sometimes I say wheeeeee and then moan; then I laugh at all of it. Saying wheeeeee wakes me up, reminding me not to take my aches and pains so seriously. It is a noise that a person makes while rolling down a hill.

Alive

by Blaze Ardman

Predawn.
I wake up surprised
and grateful for another chance.

This body –
which at times,
(between sporadic intervals of care)
in service of causes worthy or not,
from boredom, or habit,
determined rebellion or
a hundred unknown reasons, or none,

has been overfed, undernourished,
underexercised and underslept,
unappreciated, too-often scorned,
too-long sat, too-little danced,
contorted into high heels,
drunken and drugged,
smushed into airplane seats,
frozen by loss,
broken by falls from bicycles and horses and skis,
tortured by tweezers,
traumatized by scalpels,
scarred by telling lies –
this body
continues to provide.

150

Mended by laughter and music,
and visitors doing
what needed to be done,
hugged and healed
with love of family and friends
lit by the rainbow of the universe,

this body still breathes me,
moves me, thinks me,
extends me, holds me,
is/is not all of or only me.
Tastes and is tasted,
sees and is made visible,
listens and is given voice,
reaches out and is touched.

Quickens to the sultry scent
of Jasmine.

Having done nothing,
no deserving or undeserving thing,
I am inexplicably blessed.

And I pray that
when yet another
random accident
or illness,
flash-flood
or slow-gathering cloud,
drenches this finite physicality

or when it's merely
time to leave it,

a moment will come
when a thousand
thundering expressions
of anger, fear, and sadness
are quieted,
an instant when pain
yields to the gentle rain of
mercy inviting me

to stop...
remember...
and say
"thank you."

Teaching
to Question

Introduction
by Gregg Krech

In my first book on Naikan reflection *(Naikan: Gratitude, Grace and the Japanese Art of Self-Reflection*, Stone Bridge Press, 2002), there is a section in the appendix in which I contrast traditional counseling to an approach grounded in self-reflection. I won't repeat the discussion here, but simply list the main elements of this comparison below and refer you to that book for additional discussion.

Contrasting Traditional Therapy and Naikan Practices

TRADITIONAL THERAPY	NAIKAN
Focus on Feelings	Focus on Facts
Revisit how the client has been hurt or mistreated in the past	Revisit how the client has been supported or cared for in the past
The therapist validates the client's experience	The therapist helps the client to understand the experience of others
The therapist acknowledges and often shows support for the client's blaming of others for her problems	The therapist helps the client take responsibility for his own conduct and how he caused problems for others
The therapist provides analysis and interpretation of the client's experience	The therapist provides a structured framework for the client's own self-reflection
The therapist helps the client increase self-esteem	The therapist helps the client increase appreciation for life and the support of others

As you can see, there are dramatic differences in these approaches, based on contrasting assumptions of how to be helpful to the client. I would suggest that there are key obstacles to overcome for anyone who wants to use Naikan from a teaching our counseling perspective.

Our Need to Analyze or Interpret the Client's Reflections

The self-reflective process is really very simple. The support person (therapist/teacher/minister/guide) provides the questions to the person who is reflecting (client/student). The subject of the person's reflection and the time period to be examined are agreed upon. How this is done will be determined by the setting and context which might be a therapy session, a workshop, or a retreat. The client takes time to reflect privately and then shares what they choose to share with the support person. The support person listens attentively and then thanks the client for the privilege of hearing their reflections.

That's it. As the support person gains experience with Naikan, personally and professionally, there is a tendency to think that there is something the client doesn't see or understand. That may well be true. In fact, it's likely to be true for all of us. We go through life with blind spots and it's usually easier for others to see those blind spots than it is for us to see them in ourselves. But to communicate that, somehow, we have a more enlightened understanding of the client's situation than they do is not only arrogant, but it sends a message to the client that answers are to be found outside themselves. For the self-reflective process to maintain its integrity, it is important that everyone understands that the work that needs to be done – psychologically, emotionally, spiritually – is the domain of the person reflecting.

The capacity to reflect sincerely and honestly is limited in all of us. The capacity to remember is limited in all of us. We will get as far as we can, given our capability at this particular moment in our lives. If the client is struggling, it is fine for us to encourage them, to clarify the questions, or even to offer, from time to time, genuine examples from our own life. But it is not our job to enter into a dialogue in which we offer our own analysis or interpretation of the client's reflections. To do so is actually
158

a distraction for the client and a subtle, or not-so-subtle, message that we know more than they do. We don't.

Our Inclination to Judge the Client

As we listen to the client share their Naikan reflections, we are likely to hear some of the terrible things they've done to others as a response to question three. Examples of such conduct might include marital affairs, physical abuse, cheating, accidents caused by drunk driving, assault, misappropriation of funds, lying, slandering, theft, neglect of children or aging parents, deception, and more. In the face of such confessions, the main defense we have against self-righteous judgment is an authentic awareness of our own transgressions. When we are intimately familiar with our own transgressions and selfish conduct, we are more likely to encounter these same types of behavior in others with understanding and acceptance. This is why it is essential that anyone who wishes to use Naikan for teaching or counseling must first go through an exhaustive examination of their own lives using the Naikan method. Our acceptance of the client and their own karmic history is essential to the client's willingness to face their own past honestly and sincerely.

Our Inclination to Comfort the Client

When I did my training in Japan, I reached a point in my own reflections which was extremely painful – not because of what others had done to me, but because I was broken-hearted over how I had treated others. The response of the person across from me to my expression of pain was . . . quiet. There were no comforting words for me or reassurance or attempts to make me feel better about myself. When I cried I was gently offered a tissue. Naikan is about seeing. If what we see makes us feel guilty, or sad, or deeply disappointed in ourselves, we need to sit with that experience. It is not the job of the counselor, teacher or guide to try to buffer such an experience. We allow people to feel joy and gratitude. We allow them to feel guilt and pain. The experience of the client is authentic and not for us to meddle with.

159

Our Desire to Lead the Client to a Place of Gratitude, Safety or Healing

When we work with someone and support them in their Naikan practice, we develop genuine concern for their happiness and a desire to see them "succeed" in the reflective process. We can be inclined to try to persuade them to make a shift in their thinking. For example, we may want to really encourage them to appreciate what they seem to be missing or ignoring. Some clients have a long history of complaining and blaming (which may have been reinforced in certain types of therapy). They may not find the transition to appreciation and assuming responsibility to be an easy one. We offer them the questions and support in the reflective process. But we cannot lead them to where they don't want to go. If there is an opportunity to see the grace or gift in a situation, it is for them to find it, not for us to try to take them there.

Conclusion

The reflective process is a mysterious process. After nearly 30 years, I do not pretend to understand it, but I have developed a great respect for it. In many ways, the role of the support person (therapist, minister, teacher, or guide) is not to get in the way of the process. Certainly, there are skills involved. We may need to help the client understand the meaning and purpose of the questions. Listening, not just superficially, but with an open heart is important. Communicating a sense of respect for the person reflecting and avoiding sending messages of self-righteousness or superiority is essential. Finally, there should be a natural humility that is anchored in the awareness that what they are doing requires much more courage and discipline than what we are doing.

160

Naikan as Preparation for Marriage in the Christian Tradition: A Case Study

by Rev. Denise Mosher

T he goal of marriage preparation within the Christian tradition is to help prepare a couple for marriage "based on a model of sacrificial love, grace and forgiveness of Jesus Christ." Christian marriage, therefore, is not a contract, but a covenant. It is not based on getting our needs met or staying together as long as our spouse continues to make us happy. It is grounded in service to the other that stands the test of time, fleeting moods and ever-changing emotions.

Yet the way the majority of Western clergy have been trained to help prepare couples for marriage does not model the Church's theology of marriage. For almost a decade I have been utilizing a highly regarded, accurate, and well implemented premarital inventory, which offers the couple and celebrant very accurate potential "red flags" and strengths of the relationship. Over these years I have asked couples to discuss points of disagreement; share relationship strengths and growth areas; practice active listening, assertiveness, and conflict resolution; share couple and relationship goals; and prepare a family budget.

Using this model I have helped perpetuate the notion that marriage is a contract and that expressing feelings and good communication builds a strong marriage. I no longer believe this. If Jesus is the theological core of Christian marriage, then I believe we need to be more like him in how we model marriage preparation.

In late 2004, I received a call from a former student I knew from my campus ministry days in Madison, Wisconsin. Tracy had been a core member of this student group and still spoke fondly of its impact on her life. She and her fiancé, Robert, live in Milwaukee and asked me to officiate at the wedding in September 2005. I joyously accepted, and we agreed to do all premarital conversation over the phone.

Robert, 26, was finishing his last year of law school and taking the Bar Exam in August. Tracy, also 26, worked in marketing and is a Reservist in the Army National

Guard. They began dating during their freshman year of high school, attended separate colleges, conducted a long-distance relationship, and began living together the year they both graduated from college. Tracy was very active in campus ministry while in college. Robert was not. Neither attends church. Tracy's positive experience with campus ministry makes her more open to religion and spirituality, while Robert is more of a skeptic and unsure of the role of faith in his life.

I met with them three times over the phone over a period of six weeks. My norm is to meet for six sessions, but this was impossible due to their responsibilities and busy schedules. Each had a strong desire to build a happy and healthy marriage, deepen an already strong bond and avoid the mistake of their parents' failed marriages, which ended in divorce. At the beginning of our work together, both Robert and Tracy expressed an interest in finding out "what was on the bubble sheets"— their premarital inventory. I told them I had a new way of talking about marriage together, Naikan reflection, which was working powerfully in my own marriage. Robert and Tracy agreed to give Naikan a try. That week, I mailed them sheets to practice with and create a Naikan journal.

In our first session, Tracy indicated that "the sheets were empty." I began sharing more about Naikan — the power of self-reflection within a marriage, how it helps to open our eyes to how things really are and not how we think or feel they are. The regular practice of Naikan in regard to our partner helps put things in perspective as we see the care they provide, while humbling us as to how we inconvenience them. I asked Tracy and Robert if the day-to-day busyness of their lives makes it difficult for them to see how things really are, especially in conflict. Both laughed and said, yes, busy lives plus conflict often lead to escalation of arguments. It really hit a chord when I asked them if they'd ever thought or said "if you'd only" to their partner: "Yeah, if he'd only do this or if he'd only do that, then I'm sure all would be perfect," Tracy joked knowingly. Robert, too, said focusing on the seeming imperfections of the other and trying to "fix their faults" didn't resolve conflict and often made matters worse. I shared more of my experience of a Naikan retreat, my husband Paul's reaction ("You should have done this ten years ago—you're so grateful"), and the three Naikan questions:

1. *What have I received?*
2. *What have I given?*
3. *What troubles or difficulties have I caused?*

After I concluded the session I asked Tracy and Robert to reflect on each other every evening using the journal sheets I had mailed them. In addition, by email, I gave Robert the assignment to do a secret service for Tracy and asked Tracy to say thank you to Robert ten times that week for specific things he did for her. (A secret service is something you do for the other without them knowing it.)

Before hanging up the phone, Tracy asked to speak to me alone, without Robert on the line. I learned that her National Guard unit had been mobilized to Iraq. The day after they returned from their honeymoon, she would leave for Mississippi for training. Then she was to report to Baghdad for one and a half years of service. This news quickly changed the context of the wedding—and my deep love and care for them as a couple.

In our second session a week later, Robert and Tracy shared their experience of doing daily Naikan on each other. I asked the question, "What have you learned about each other by practicing Naikan reflection?"

"It's confirmed even more so that I want to marry Tracy. She does so much for me. She is probably the sweetest person I've ever met…"

"Naikan helps me focus away from what I usually think about: what's going wrong, what he could do differently. I see what Robert does for me. The list is huge!"

Our third session was dedicated to planning the wedding service, talking more about the impact of the mobilization to Iraq on their marriage and touching base about Naikan. Both Tracy and Robert reported that they very much enjoyed doing daily Naikan: "We like it so much; it makes us see the great things about the other and be so grateful that we want to take our worksheets on the honeymoon and continue doing Naikan." They also both agreed that they benefited greatly from the style and ethos of

163

sharing Naikan as a means to premarital counseling.

"We love the way you ask us what we experienced, what we thought when doing Naikan," Tracy said. "It just felt so respectful rather than you telling us—it led to some wonderful, sharing conversations."

The Naikan experience and sharing sessions together created a bridge of trust and care that would not have occurred with my previous method of marriage preparation. At an emotional goodbye party, just before leaving for the airport, I asked the couple if I could say a blessing for them and for Tracy's safety in Iraq. Both warmly agreed. While blessing their foreheads in prayer, I saw in their eyes deep love for each other and trust in me. In this, of course, I am the one blessed. My own marriage has been renewed in the presence of their love.

Naikan immediately helped create a space where Robert and Tracy could care for each other, seeing the amazing gifts and truth about their partner's love, even within conflict. Additionally, Naikan helped each of them shift their attention away from the "missing fourth question" of Naikan—what you do to cause trouble to me (or as I said to them in our first session "how you drive me nuts!").

In the Christian tradition, humility is a fundamental virtue. Sadly, much of the marriage preparation in which Western clergy are trained ignores humility altogether. Traditional Western premarital counseling often focuses on assertiveness skills (asking for what you want) and active listening (listening to one's partner asking for what they want) or self-esteem.

Additionally "being humble" is often stated as a virtue without addressing what this means or tools to practice it in daily life.

Naikan reflection is a gentle, yet effective, tool to chip away at the reality we subscribe to, providing greater insight about how the world really is rather than how we think it is. We are greatly loved. Our mates do incredible things for us. We literally walk on grace and love every day. And to the Christian tradition this is essential: We are loved not because of what we do or who we are but because Christ has, like a medic in a field full of land mines, come to heal and wrap our wounds. This is a model for marriage to which the Church can aspire.

House Calls
by Robert Strayhan, M.D.

I am a psychiatric physician who provides integrative medical care for my patients. I have done what you might call field work, when working with the chronically mentally ill as well as mentally ill offenders. I have visited crack houses and prisons to bring needed care to my patients. I have gone under bridges to deliver care, when necessary.

I am not trying to make myself appear special. The tradition of house calls has been a noble and accepted one up until the last few decades. In the past, physicians were seen as tired healers with black bags in hand and a stethoscope hanging from their necks. They made the rounds to see those who could not come to the office for any number of reasons. But one, often overlooked, reason was to assess the environment in which the patient functioned. This provided the doctor with an idea of the patient's daily life —one that was not easily discernable during an office visit.

This is one of the main reasons that "Naikan reflection" is in my "little black bag". All too often, families are distanced from each other by busy schedules and the technology that allows them to keep in touch without really connecting. Most families don't sit at a table together for the evening meal. Why spend time speaking to each other when you can text?

Many people take for granted the family's dependence on one another and feel entitled to the support and help they're receiving. There is a sense of "This is what my father is supposed to do" or "This is what my wife is supposed to do." There is very little room, without some inward reflection, to feel and express gratitude for the many needs and privileges the family provides. This is why, in clinically appropriate cases and with informed consent, I sometimes use Naikan therapy for a member of a couple who may feel undervalued within the relationship.

As an example, let me discuss a gentleman who grew up in the rural South, subsisting on a hand-to-mouth existence. He did not have a college education; however, he rose to financial success through hard work and by being much smarter on a functional level than his academic background suggested. He married a beautiful woman who was both strong in spirit and mind – a woman who supported him through good times and bad. But lately he felt his wife was not grateful for the material things that he had provided to her. He felt as if his wife and teenaged daughter were allied against him to undercut his authority as "the man of the house." He complained frequently in individual psychotherapy sessions about how alone and isolated he felt at home – how he often felt taken for granted.

I believed this was the perfect opportunity for the application of Naikan reflection. Rather than make it an intellectual exercise, I offered to provide the experience of Naikan in his home. He was interested and agreed. He discussed the possibility of a "Naikan house call" with his wife, and she also agreed it was a good idea. I then explained the process to them and they eagerly helped make arrangements that would be most conducive to an optimal outcome.

We planned the Naikan experience for a Saturday and they were advised that the experience would last from 8AM to 5PM. They had a shoji screen at home, and the husband would remain secluded behind the screen for the day. They agreed to have their daughter spend the day with friends. They also agreed not to answer the phone or use electronic communication devices or computers during the daylong exercise. The wife would prepare meals for her husband while he was in seclusion.

During the day of Naikan, I met with the husband regularly and assigned him periods of time to reflect on in his marriage. Meals were served at the designated times, and midway through the day, he was given the opportunity to walk outside for 15 minutes. He was advised not to speak to anyone during the walk. Towards the end of the day, he was given an opportunity to write himself a letter describing where he wanted to be in life three months later. The letter was placed in a self-addressed envelope and given to me to mail to him at some time in the future.

The most striking change that took place over the course of the day was how he began to see how his wife had been supporting him every step of the way. He also began to see how he had offered her material support in place of the love and affection she so desperately wanted from him.

He recognized that his family was often too busy to sit down and eat meals together. But, more importantly, he was able to reflect on the effort that went into the meal preparation. He realized the attention to detail and caring that went into making a meal that was not only nutritious but appealing to the eye. He began to comment consistently about how much of his family life he missed while trying to "bring home the bacon" and be the man of the house. He saw how much he was trying to control his relationships with his wife and daughter and how he felt entitled to respect as a father and husband, even though he hadn't really earned that respect. None of these conclusions came from me. They came from his sincere and fearless inward looking during his process of quiet self-reflection.

He was no longer a victim, but neither did he assume the guilty role of perpetrator. He began to think that maybe everyone was doing the best they could under the circumstances. And those circumstances could be better if he was more involved in the daily functions of the family. He realized that, too often, he had been "missing in action" as a husband and father.

After the Naikan experience was over, I had both spouses sit on the couch together and asked if they felt comfortable touching each other as they offered their individual perspectives of how the day went. I suggested the daughter spend the night with her friends to give them more time to process the experience. They agreed, and later spent the evening dining out and going to a movie.

When I followed up with the husband, he told me how much the experience had impacted his life, and that he now does Naikan regularly. He admits things aren't perfect, but he realizes that they don't have to be in order for him to be happy.

Several months later, I met with the couple and they commented on how good the experience had been for their relationship. They even wondered if the wife might have an opportunity to experience what happens behind the shoji screen. But we all laughed – take-out meals would be necessary, as the husband could barely boil water and his attempts to cook food could be hazardous to her health.

Naikan is not a cure-all, nor is it intended to be. But, as a doctor, I find it is one of the most potent treatments I have in my "little black bag."

Naikan and Psychotherapy

by Gregory Willms

When I was first introduced to Naikan, I was asked to write a letter to an aunt with whom I was upset, thanking her for three specific things I received and apologizing for three things I had done to cause her trouble. This seemingly simple assignment proved to be extremely powerful in reminding me of the much wider context of my relationship with my aunt, a context in which my grievances suddenly seemed small and petty. Later, I began formal reflection on my mother, looking for answers to each of Naikan's three questions. These first experiences with Naikan were profound, and they left me with the need to more fully examine my life. I attended a seven-day Naikan retreat and later assisted in organizing and leading two Naikan retreats where I was able to listen to the Naikan reflection of others. These rich experiences have fundamentally changed my perception of life.

One of my goals is to make Naikan reflection available to others and I have found it to be extremely helpful to clients who come for psychotherapy. Too frequently, clients only expect therapy to provide a safe place for them to explore the trouble and bother others have caused them. Naikan reflection can be a skillful way of restoring balance to the client's perceptions. As a therapist, I keep these questions in mind and look for opportunities to focus attention on what has been received, what has been given, and the troubles and difficulties caused others.

I often ask clients to bring family photographs which can stimulate memories and help direct attention to the Naikan questions. For example, I have asked clients where the toys in the picture came from, who paid for summer camp, or how they got to and from the school play. My favorite question is, "Who took this picture?" In my experience, such a casual look at pictures widens the client's perspective on his or her past.

After just such a session, reflecting on photos of her mother, one client reported, "What I realized was that she was there for me a hundred percent. In who she was, she was there for me absolutely. And who I wanted was somebody else's mother. I wanted Pammy's mother. I wanted Angie's mother. I realize now that she gave to me from who she was." Much of the pain we carry is caused by comparing our childhood and parents with some imagined ideal of a perfect childhood and perfect parenting. Naikan can be an effective tool to help us attend, moment to moment, to what we actually did receive.

Frequently, I will ask clients to write a letter, especially to a person with whom they are having difficulty, thanking them specifically for what was received and apologizing for the particular troubles they caused. The client may decide whether or not to send the letter, but in either case the process of writing provides an opportunity for Naikan reflection. The following letter was written by a woman to her ex-husband after a difficult divorce:

Dear Jim,

Thank you for taking care of me after our daughter Sierra was born. I remember the breakfast you served me in bed. It was delicious. Thank you for massaging my neck when it flared up; it always made my neck feel better when you worked on it.

Naikan is also helpful to those suffering from obsessional thinking. In speaking about her ex-boyfriend, one woman noted,

"When he would come to mind, rather than go with my anger or my fantasies about him and the other woman – obsessing about all that – I would turn it around to the three questions so that I could look at a more balanced picture. I looked at the periods of our daily life together: the beginning, then when things were okay, then when it was coming apart. Before Naikan, when I was angry about us splitting up, I was the angel and he was the devil. Now I see so much more. I remember him going out in the storming rain to get our wood from the wood pile, and I'd just be lying on the couch."

Naikan helps to restore two-dimensional black and white caricatures to real, three-dimensional people.

One woman put Naikan to particularly good use. She came to see me because a serious back injury had stopped her from almost all activity and she felt her life was ending. I asked her to reflect on her body, and to write it a letter of apology and thanks:

My Dear Body,

I am ashamed by my lack of love and consideration for you. I have spent virtually the whole time I have occupied you either hating the way you look, cursing your limitations, or driving you to bend to my preferences and desires. I have never listened to you unless I liked what you were saying. To get my attention you had to literally quit functioning. I am sorry.

Body, I want to thank you for being such a well-built home. Your immune system has been a great, efficient protector on which I can always depend, and your ability to heal, grow and adapt is a miracle. Thank you for housing my children and safely birthing and nurturing them. Thank you for breathing. Thank you for your hearty appetite and your efficient way of metabolizing food. I am indeed thankful for your service and the spirit within.

The same woman recalled, "*I remember laying on the floor in my living room and watching the plum tree in my front yard blossom. I had always wanted to be in my house in the morning with the sun pouring through the window, watching the blossoms on that tree. Well, here was my opportunity to have that.*"

In the therapeutic setting, Naikan reflection naturally cycles with action. As Thich Nhat Hanh has said,

"*Once there is seeing, there must be acting. Otherwise, what is the use of seeing?*"
A client said, "*I did Naikan on my house. It's taken really good care of me, really given me a lot. I just stayed there and let it take care of me. But with Naikan, my attention shifted to what I could do for the house.*"

I find this natural interplay between reflection and action to be at the heart of good therapy and of good living. Naikan's three questions attend to behavior, rather than feelings or thoughts. The ways in which we benefit from the actions of others and the impact of our actions on the lives of others becomes clear.

One of my clients expressed long-standing envy of her sister's marriage, children, and security. In "putting the three questions to herself", she saw many specific instances in which her sister had been helpful to her, and many incidents of trouble she has caused. I suggested she organize a surprise dinner for her sister on Mother's Day. She did and reported,

"I realize that in not just saying thank you, but in actually taking action, in doing something concrete, that my sister got it, and that others in the family could participate too. It's shifted how I think about her."

Action also leads to reflection. The client who had suffered a back injury was later involved in a car accident. To keep her sanity, she said, she first kept her attention focused on what needed to be done next. That evening, at home with her daughter, she reflected on the wonder of being alive, sitting on the couch, drinking soup. Action-Reflection-Action. As this client said,

"In one hand you have the tool of Naikan and in the other you have the tool of action, of doing what needs to be done. You just use those two lights to shine your way through life."

Naikan with Prisoners
by Yoshinori Sato

I recently worked with a man who has been confined in a solitary unit of prison due to his serious anger and violent behavior. The use of Naikan was relatively easy and straightforward because he was already in the stage of contemplation and generally amenable to psychological treatment. I introduced the Naikan method and had him reflect on the questions as they relate to the current day –

What did I receive from the world today? What did I give to the world today? What troubles and difficulties did I cause to the world today?

There were two main objectives for utilizing this method in his therapy:

1. To cultivate gratitude by recognizing that people are still supporting him, despite all the troubles/difficulties he has caused. For example, his mother is still contacting him and taxpayers are providing him with food and necessities;

2. To become compassionate by realizing that he is not in a position to become angry and judgmental toward others who provoke him because he has done something similar, or much worse, to others in the past.

Even with a single session, the outcome of this intervention was more than what I expected. This man was able to show appreciation for his family, society, and even staff, including guards, for supports he has been receiving. Furthermore, he was able to verbalize, with remorse, that he has harmed others and it is necessary for him to be humble and not react with anger when he is disrespected or provoked by others.

I think Naikan is a very potent and effective therapy technique with a very wide applicability – ranging from self-development to the rehabilitation of felons. I am also convinced, based on my personal experience with Naikan reflection and the evidence from the actual applications in my clinical practice, that Naikan may be more effective than other methods. I believe that the clinical applications of Naikan therapy need to be further investigated.

Life Coaching: Improving Relationships through Naikan Self-Reflection

by Viveca Monahan

In my work as a life coach I often introduce Naikan as a tool to help the client go deeper into self-reflection, especially when there may be unresolved relationship issues. Often, someone will be carrying deep-seated emotions about a family member, friend, or other significant person. This relationship challenge may be holding them back from realizing a life goal. It is not in the purview of a coach to counsel, provide therapy or otherwise probe and analyze around a client's past. Coaching focuses on the present and future. Even so, when a client feels stuck because she has identified a relationship challenge, it is useful to pause and focus on the challenge. This is when I might offer Naikan as a method for the client to do some personal reflection.

My client, "Mary," was considering a trip cross country for a family reunion. In her seventies, one of Mary's goals was to visit her estranged family members, but she was held back by the thought of seeing her older brother, Glenn, whom she hadn't seen in over twenty years. She was angry with him for how bossy and mean-spirited he had been to her and other family members. He was argumentative, critical and often said deeply hurtful things.

One of Mary's highest values was authenticity. She didn't want to show up at the reunion with a superficial attitude, harboring anger and bitterness. She wanted to go with a genuinely light heart and enjoy her experience despite what she knew would be Glenn's negative presence. I asked Mary if she would be willing to try a process of self-reflection that could help her with how she viewed her relationship with her brother. I asked her to remember back to a time when they were children – five or six years old. I offered her the three core questions that provide a basis for self-reflection. What had she received from her brother? What had she given to him? What troubles and difficulties had she caused him?

Mary took the Naikan home with her and the next time we met she told me

175

she spent four hours with it. She recalled so many kindnesses from him, yet she couldn't recall more than a few things she gave in return. She also considered the troubles she caused him when they were children, by crying, screaming, and tattling. This was not about forgiving him for his mean-spirited behavior or his bullying or his neglect. It was about her remembering what else was true about her relationship with him. Reality has so many sides to it. Mary's willingness to see what else was true about her brother changed her attitude about attending the reunion and seeing him. She considered, for the first time, what it was like to be Glenn, the oldest of seven children whose father left them all at a young age. How did he feel? What had been his sorrows?

Mary did attend the reunion. When she entered the house, the first words she heard were Glenn's. He was shouting across the room "It's about time you got here. You never could be on time!" In the past Mary would have felt humiliated and angry. Then she would have seethed all evening. This time she decided to roll with him. "I see you haven't changed either, Glenn!" Then she walked up to him, dropped her bags, and gave him a hug. He was speechless.

Glenn, once back in control of his tongue, told Mary that her hair style made her look old. Mary reminded him she was old. And so was he. It went on like that for the weekend. Glenn continued his criticizing and Mary handed it back. She had a lovely time with the rest of the family, and found a few hours to sit with Glenn and tell him about some of her memories of when they were little kids. Glenn went into a long rant about their lousy father who walked out on his family 65 years ago. Mary agreed. He was a lousy father. She also wondered what else might be true of him.

Mary returned from her journey with the satisfaction of reaching an important goal: She reunited with her family. She also realized that by focusing solely on Glenn's negative traits she was confirming her own bully story about him. When she opened herself up to seeing what else was true about her brother, her heart softened and she began to feel a glimmer of affection, which I know grew deeper in the few years they had left together.

Naikan in the Classroom

by Amy Szarkowski

I had an experience in the classroom that I want to share. I was teaching counseling to undergraduate students at a college in Japan. Many of the students were struggling with what advice to give to clients. I have been less successful in conveying the idea that counseling is not only about giving advice, but also about creating a space for clients to explore issues and to build a safe and rewarding relationship.

I decided to have the students read "What is Naikan?" from the ToDo Institute's website. In a group, we discussed the purpose of thinking in terms of gratitude, and we reflected on what the class members thought might be the benefits of the Naikan approach. We chose nature as our topic, since we wanted a collective theme to reflect upon. The list created by the students looked something like this:

What has nature given to us?

Mountains
Trees
Water
Food
Animals
Beauty
Relaxation
Comfort
Inspiration
Beaches
Solitude
Plants
Wind

Sun
Air
Health
Awe
Rain
Art
Interconnectedness
Life

What have we given to nature?
Recycling
Plant flowers/trees
Making good transportation choices (bike instead of drive, walk when possible, etc.)
Letter writing on behalf of the environment
Protection
Litter Clean-up

What have we done to harm or cause trouble to nature?
Global warming
Pollution
Rising sea levels
Destruction
Deforestation
Lack of protection
Extinction of animals and plants

As a result of this exercise, several students were moved to tears – not something I have often seen in Japan. Three students asked me if they could redo their homework assignment for the day to include more ideas of gratitude. Five students stayed after class and discussed ways they could become more involved in "paying back" nature. One student, who had just been assigned as my tutee for her senior thesis, asked if she could change her topic and write, instead, about gratitude and the impact it can have on people. Another student, a member of the student activist group at this college, contacted her thesis advisor and asked the same thing. Two more students stopped in my office and said they wanted to do Naikan reflection on each of their parents. And a student who has never spoken in class unless called upon raised his hand and shared his experience of reflecting on nature.

The power of reflection is amazing. I am grateful to my students for showing me this power so directly. I feel inspired.

The Pizza Party Team
by Kiki Latimer

I teach a six-week course called "Silence & Solitude" to adults at the Osher Life Long Learning Institute (OLLI) at the University of Rhode Island. This course is an introduction to silence, awareness, breath and solitude. Each class is designed to explore the meaning, value, and forms of taking silence into our lives. We delve into both the reasons for silence and the practical issues of how to do it.

In my most recent course, I decided to try a group activity based on a subchapter in the book *Naikan: Gratitude, Grace and the Japanese Art of Self-Reflection* called "Ordering a Pizza." This section invites us to reflect on how many people are involved in your receiving a pizza at your door, from the growers of the tomatoes and grain for the sauce and crust to the making of the ovens to cook it in and the car the delivery person uses to get to your house.

I broke the class into six groups, and each group was asked to make a list of no less than 30 people's jobs their pizza required:

1. *Starting with the tomato seeds, make a list of all the jobs required to create a jar of pizza tomato sauce (Don't forget spices & packaging);*
2. *Starting with the cow, make a list of all the jobs required to make a pound of mozzarella cheese (Don't forget packaging);*
3. *Starting with the grain of wheat, make a list of all the jobs required to make a pound of pizza dough (Don't forget the oil, yeast, salt);*
4. *Starting with the foundation, make a list of all the jobs required to make a pizza store (Don't forget utilities);*
5. *Starting with a tree, make a list of all the jobs required to make a pizza box (Don't forget the writing on it and design);*
6. *Starting with a spark plug, make a list of all the jobs required to make a delivery vehicle that can be used for someone to deliver a pizza (Don't forget gas).*

I gave the class about fifteen minutes to work on their list. Then, group by group, they read me their list aloud and I put the results on the white board under each category. It soon became apparent that even though we only scratched the surface of whom was involved under each category, thousands of persons were involved in getting that pizza from the farm to our doorstep!

I think that for all involved in this assignment it was an eye-opening experience. No one had ever really considered such things before in such detail and clarity. As Gregg Krech writes, we "cannot help but be deeply touched by all the effort that went into bringing me a pizza."

This was a wonderful activity to help a group to connect with the concept of gratitude and how much we take for granted on a daily basis. It was fun and interactive while at the same time being deeply personal and meaningful.

Where and How
to Practice
Self-Reflection

Introduction:
How to Practice Naikan Reflection at Home
by Gregg Krech

E ven short periods of time for self-reflection can have a significant impact your life and your relationships. It can help cultivate a deep sense of gratitude for how you are supported and inspire you to develop a deeper understanding of others and greater compassion for their difficulties.

Where:

Choose a quiet place where you will have few distractions. A meditation cushion, a comfortable chair, or a quiet spot in nature will do. Try to create an arrangement where you limit distractions in your visual field. Sometimes, however, an opportunity may arise to reflect during the course of your day – for example, in a doctor's waiting room or while waiting for a friend to meet you for lunch. One of my favorite places to reflect is on an airplane coming back from a trip. You simply work with whatever conditions are available.

When:

If you're doing daily Naikan reflection, it is best to wait till the end of the day just before bedtime. If you are reflecting on your relationship with another person, it can be done at any time. How much time does it take? For daily Naikan, take 20-30 minutes. For reflection on another person, 50-60 minutes is ideal. During the course of the day, you can simply take 2-3 minutes to reflect when such opportunities arise.

What to Do:

The core of Naikan reflection is based on three questions.

What did I receive from _____?
What did I give to _____?
What troubles and difficulties did I cause _____?

Use a journal or a blank sheet of paper divided into three columns. Answer each question, devoting at least 50% of the time to question three and dividing the remaining time between questions one and two. Do your best to answer in concrete detail and not generalizations. Instead of writing "my friend provided support when I was upset" write what your friend actually did − "came over to my apartment for 2 hours, listened to me talk about my problems, made me a cup of tea, reassured me that things would be OK, helped me fold my laundry", etc.

Let's begin our inquiry with the first question:

What have I received from _____?

To examine your relationship with another, begin by looking at what you have received from that person. My wife made me fresh-squeezed orange juice this morning. She washed my breakfast dishes. She gave me the watch I'm wearing. These are all simple, clear descriptions of reality. Her attitude or motivation does not change the fact that I benefited from her effort.

So please take a few minutes and begin making a list of what you've received during the past 24 hours in detail. This type of daily reflection is called "Daily Naikan" *(nichijo naikan)*. You are not limited to examining your relationship to one person, but can include anyone who supported you during the past day. Be specific and write down as many items as you can remember. What kind of food did you eat? Where did you go this past day? How did others support you? Did someone open a door? Did someone wash your dishes, or was there soap available to you for washing dishes? What made it possible for you to brush your teeth or drive a car? Make as thorough a list as possible. As you list what you have received from another person, you become grounded in the simple reality of how you have been supported and cared for. Your heart/mind begin to open to the compassion that underlies all life.

Please continue to the second question:

What have I given to _____?

Take another ten minutes and make a list of what you have given to others during the past 24 hours. Perhaps you gave someone a ride or prepared their dinner. Perhaps you sent a birthday card to a friend or picked up some litter on the street. Once again, be concrete and specific. Try to avoid generalizations like "I was helpful" or "I was very supportive." What did you actually do for others? What did you actually give? Ishin Yoshimoto (the founder of this method) was a businessman. Each month he would send statements to his customers and receive similar statements from suppliers. These statements specified the products that were delivered and the amount of money received. We receive a similar statement from the bank regarding our checking account. It tells us the precise balance in our account. Yoshimoto believed it was useful for human beings to conduct a similar examination or "life reconciliation." When you have examined, in detail, what you have given and received, you can determine the balance. You can compare your giving (credits) and taking (debits) in relation to a single person or between you and the rest of the world.

This process is both a practical and spiritual reconciliation of our relationships with others. Does the world owe me, or do I owe the world? Am I in debt to my mother, or is she in debt to me? We often live our life as if the world owes us. "Why didn't I get that raise?" "Why is the pizza so late?" "How come I don't get more appreciation from my boss?" We resent it when people do not fulfill our expectations, and live as if we deserve whatever we desire. When people do support us, we often take their efforts for granted, living as if we were entitled to their support. Suppose I discover that I am the one who is in debt to the world. Such a realization kindles a natural desire to give and serve others and instills in me a greater sense of gratitude and realistic humility.

The third and final question is the most difficult of all:

What troubles or difficulties have I caused others?

Now please take another ten minutes and make a list of the troubles and difficulties you have caused others in the past 24 hours. Did you criticize someone? Did you leave dishes in the sink for someone else to wash? Did you keep someone waiting for a response to an email or telephone call? Were you late for an appointment? Once again, please be specific.

Mostly we are aware of how other people cause us inconvenience or difficulty. Perhaps somebody cuts us off in traffic, or maybe the person in front of us at the post office has a lot of packages and we are kept waiting. We notice such incidents with great proficiency. But when we are the source of the trouble or inconvenience, we often don't notice it at all. If we do, we think, "it was an accident" or "I didn't mean it." Perhaps we simply dismiss it as "not such a big deal."

The third question is very important. Yoshimoto suggested that when we reflect on ourselves, we should spend at least 60 percent of the time considering how we have caused others trouble. His words are echoed by the lives of Franklin, Schweitzer, and St. Augustine. If we are not willing to see and accept those events in which we have been the source of others' suffering, then we cannot truly know ourselves or the grace by which we live.

Who Should You Reflect On?

If you're reflecting on another person, it can be someone who has played a meaningful role in your life – mother, father, sibling, spouse, good friend, teacher, colleague, supervisor, etc. Avoid reflecting on the entire duration of your relationship with the person unless you've only known them for less than six months. Instead, divide up the relationship into increments of years or months and begin by reflecting on the earliest period. When reflecting on your spouse, you might start by reflecting on the period prior to marriage when you were dating.

After You're Done:

Sit quietly for a few minutes and review what you have written. Look honestly at the items in each list. In Japan, it is common to share your reflection with a person who has experience with Naikan (called mensetsu), but you can share it with a friend or spouse if you are both interested in developing a regular practice. If you have an opportunity to listen to someone else's reflection, just be attentive and listen with an open heart – don't offer comments or advice in response.

Naikan, as a method of self-reflection, is about seeing, about awareness. It does not prescribe that you take any action or do anything. However, as you review your reflection, you can ask yourself the question, "Is there something I need to do?" You may have a natural response to this question in light of your reflection. For example, you may decide to write a letter, offer an apology, offer an amends, or give a gift. Or you may decide that there is nothing to do. In any case, you simply allow any action to emerge naturally in light of your awareness.

The questions themselves seem rather simple. The depth of experience, insight, and realization that comes from the practice of self-reflection is not a result of intellectual analysis or complex theories. Our challenge is just to see reality as it is. These questions are simple inquiries for our investigation of life's mysteries and miracles.

The Retreat of a Lifetime
by Margarita Delgado Creamer

The room was filled with the warm light of dusk. It was still winter but the light and the room felt delightfully warm. Or so I remember it.

I had so many misgivings about the retreat: would they serve coffee in the morning? Would there be enough food or would we be subjected to an all too frugal Japanese diet? What if I got hungry mid-morning? Would I remember enough? And, above all, the silence. Not speaking, no music, would I be able to bear this kind of mandated silence?

When we arrived Hogen and his wife, Eiho, welcomed us. They would be two of our four *mensetsusha* (the people who staff the retreat). The woman, Eiho, with a slim figure and penetrating small eyes, would untiringly labor to feed us and keep the retreat running smoothly. Hogen was a man whose age I cannot guess, and whose dark eyes under thick grey eyebrows looked at us with infinite kindness. He showed me the room where I would stay for the week. It had a cave inside! Well, something akin to a cave, a space where I could only fit in sitting position. There were two meditation cushions there. The space had been lovingly arranged as if to assuage my anxiety. I felt like a child ready to play hide and seek.

I return to the "cave" at times. I sit on the blue cushion and hear the deep silence. I can breathe it. It is soothing and energizing. In that secluded and protected space I felt closer than ever before to the people I love and to those I do not even know. Like a womb, like an unborn child – up to that point I had only understood the Daoist simile analytically. Now it was pregnant with meaning and promise.

Hogen ritually greets and bows to me. He asks me to report my reflections with his forehead on his hands pressed against the bare floor. I feel embarrassed (and relieved, no judgmental eyes!). His respect and humility strike a chord that reverberates throughout my body. Memories of my mother flow and repeat themselves. I can see them as if projected on a screen. I can see myself, too, as a child but my image is blurred.

There is a degree of rawness to these memories of quotidian actions—my mother cooking, sorting the laundry, petting my dog—that transforms them into something precious, sacred and omnipresent, as if each of them infinitely multiplied in time and space. I want to be there and thank my mother with all my heart, I want to take her hands and ask her to rest. I want to be there. I want that child to turn her head and look at her mother and show her gratitude, but the child's attention is somewhere else. Was that really me?

The memories fade out. I try to recover them, but instead now I only see the cup of tea in my hands. The past can feel so uncannily present and real, and yet the effort to remember sometimes seems to make memories recede ever further.

I try to analyze, to understand what I have just experienced. I smile at myself. It is good I have another time period to reflect on. Otherwise, I would distract myself and I have barely started. I like the first question. It is like a lullaby. The second question, on the other hand, is like a wake-up call. But the third is even more disruptive. It's truly unsettling. I cannot think of a simpler and more powerful set of questions – they work in tandem. As much as I want to stay clear of the third question, I am thankful Eiho and Hogen keep reminding me that I should devote more time to it. They also cook delicious food every day. I feel at home. I remember my worries about the retreat and I laugh.

The last day John, who had flown amidst a terrible storm to serve as our *mensetsusha*, reads us the poem he had written during the retreat. I do not remember one single word. I just remember that it expressed what I had experienced, except more beautifully. I can see him reading the poem and there are no words to be heard – just a sound that resonates with the deepest silence. It was the perfect farewell.

I love travelling and living abroad, visiting beautiful places, getting to know people and their cultures. But of all my travels, this has been the most significant journey.

At first the realizations seemed painful. I never thought of myself as a troublemaker, but haven't I caused, and don't I continue to cause, so much trouble to so many living beings every day, even if I don't intend to? I had been sorely aware of the hurt others had caused me but what about the pain I have caused others? And the good things? The achievements, for instance? I thought they were all mine, earned with hard study and work. And yet could I have attained any if my father had not taken me to school, my mother prepared a succulent lunchbox every weekday, my brothers and cousins helped me with difficult homework? And there were teachers who prepared their classes and borne patiently a bunch of pampered kids. What if Ms. Dina had not held my hand the first day of my new school, and Sayda had not welcomed me as an old friend? The list is endless.

Initially, it seemed painful to recognize the debts I owe, and that I had not done anything on my own. Worst of all was that I had caused much more pain than what had been inflicted on me. But when I started to accept all of this wholeheartedly I felt a sense of empathy that revealed a world that did not revolve around me, a world akin to the Naikan room. It sounds counterintuitive, I know, but that gave me such a great relief.

I felt I was starting to rewrite my story.

The Naikan Retreat: Day by Day

by Gregg Krech and Linda Anderson Krech

DAY ONE

This is the first day of your spring Naikan Retreat. You might be at a Naikan center in Japan, surrounded by rice paddies. You might be at a center in Germany, on the border of the Bavarian forest. You might be at the ToDo Institute, at the foothills of the Green Mountains in Vermont. Wherever you are, it is likely that you have come a long way to reflect on your life . . . and to take a look at your Self.

As you begin the retreat, you are sitting on comfortable cushions, perhaps with a cup of hot tea or coffee, surrounded by Japanese shoji screens. You have been given a small card to remind you of the lens you will be looking through – the vantage point that is revealed by the following three questions:

What have I received?
What have I given?
What troubles have I caused?

You will examine these questions in relation to those who have played an important role in your life: your mother, father, siblings, partner, ex-partner, children, colleagues, teachers, best friends, and others.

Today you will be reflecting primarily on your mother (or whomever was your primary caretaker during your earliest years). Mothers are controversial beings. They bring us into this world, and proceed to keep us alive for the many years in which we are incapable of caring for ourselves. And they do it imperfectly, which we tend to notice.

Most of us disconnect with our mother when we leave home, but the way we remember our childhood years can leave its residue on the rest of our lives, with gratitude, resentment, or both.

194

When we think back on this time we do so with the advantage of time. We can see and understand things in retrospect that we wouldn't have understood at that time. It's one of the most important reasons for reflecting back on the past, particularly our early years. Otherwise we carry the understanding of an eight-year-old, or teenager, with us into our adulthood and old age.

Why not take some time for reflection on your relationship with your mom? Examine the first ten years of your life. Or maybe the turbulence of your high school years. You know, all too well, what it was like for you to have to deal with your mother. But a sincere effort of self-reflection turns the question around: What was it like for your mom to have you as her son or daughter?

Are you courageous enough to explore this question with genuine curiosity and an open heart?

DAY TWO

We're in the second day of the Naikan retreat. You've just come in from a 25-minute work period which, luckily, got sandwiched between two periods of rain today. Cold rain. The skies are gray and the temperature is just below 50 degrees F.

It doesn't sound like you would normally want to go outside in that kind of weather. But today you are looking forward to it – really looking forward to it. That's because you have spent nearly the entire day (except for a morning break) sitting behind Japanese screens, on cushions, and quietly reflecting on your father.

Whatever your view of your father is when you arrived here, it is likely to shift. Maybe he drank a lot of whiskey. Maybe he was violent. Maybe he was overbearing and strict. Or perhaps you remember him as kind, but distant. Perhaps he taught you to play sports, but pushed you too far. Or maybe he was just an all-around great dad.

When Gregg first reflected on his father, one of the things that surfaced was something that connected them for nearly 40 years. That something was cars. His dad played some kind of supportive role in nearly every car he owned for most of his life.

What was your connection to your dad? Or were you, are you, disconnected?

It's worth taking a closer look at your relationship. Take a 3 to 4 year period of time, for example, your high school years, and spend some time reflecting on the three Naikan questions:

What did you receive from your dad?
What did you give to your dad?
What troubles and difficulties did you cause your dad?

Most people are very familiar with the 4th question: What troubles and difficulties did my dad cause me?

Well …. we must sadly inform you that this question isn't part of the reflective process.

Why not? For one thing, most of us are already proficient at answering this question on a daily basis. You don't have to attend a retreat to answer this query.

But there's a second, more important reason. We'll let you ponder it, but it has to do with karmic responsibility – that's your clue.

So now, after you've come in from the work period and taken your shower, you sit back down on the cushions and suddenly are hit by an incredible aroma coming from the kitchen. What is that appetizing aroma from? You'll find out in about 30 minutes. Until then, you refocus on the questions, and your father. For now, that's all there is to do.

DAY THREE

If your partner took a magic truth potion, how would he or she describe you? What is it like to live with you, day after day? What are the joys and what are the challenges? How do you make life difficult? What habits create friction? What behaviors cause conflict? What tendencies take a toll on love?

The third day of the Naikan Retreat focuses primarily on intimate relationships. During the course of the day you'll search through those relationships from all angles — from the front door and the back door, through holidays and seasons, vacations and celebrations . . .

You'll scan your memory for answers to the Naikan questions, in your quest to better understand your partner's experience (and to recognize the blessings you received as well). You look down at your little card which reminds you of your reflective lens:

What did I receive from my partner?
What did I give to my partner?
What troubles and difficulties did I cause to my partner?

In our everyday lives we often defend, rationalize, and explain our behaviors to others and to ourselves. We may explain the context and the extenuating circumstances so that others can understand the truth, as we see it, and can continue to regard us in as positive a light as possible.

But during the retreat, we pause from those efforts in an attempt to get real. We step out of our shoes and into our partner's, as fully as possible, searching for the truth wherever we can find it.

Ironically, our best chance to be a loving and accepting partner is to recognize our own failings, shortcomings and weaknesses. Then we know that we do not deserve a perfect partner, for we are far from perfect. How far? Our willingness to look at each successive relationship gives us insight that is both disturbing, yet softening. It takes great courage and honesty to give up the banner of the innocent victim and acknowledge our own faults and shortcomings that contributed to the difficulties of these relationships.

DAY FOUR

It's 5:50am and you hear the sound of the morning bell, announcing the start of a new day. You've already been lying awake for a while, listening to the songs of the

cardinals accompanied by some chickadees and a few chattering red squirrels.
There are so many birds here, including "Claudia Cardinale" who, with fierce
determination, attacks her own beautiful, but threatening, reflection in the window
every morning. You are impressed that even the birds at the ToDo Institute are involved
with self-reflection in their own way.

The theme this morning is reflection on family members, including extended
family. You're given the choice of selecting someone. Who should you select to reflect
on – your brother, your grandmother, your aunt whom you spent summers with as a
child?

Gregg Krech, who is leading the retreat, offers a brief talk mid-morning, just
prior to your morning walk. You sit outside on the deck with the other participants.
Gregg speaks about our tendency to be self-righteous and judgmental, and he offers
the maxim, "We find compassion for others in our own transgressions."

The sun is out after two days of rain and clouds and you are especially eager
to take your walk in the woods this morning.

The afternoon theme changes to "Lying and Stealing", a theme similar to the
Buddhist precept and the ninth Christian commandment. This process involves
searching your entire life for examples of how you have violated the moral imperatives
of "not lying" and "not stealing." This is hard. It's a direct threat to your ego and your
self-righteous arrogance. You're given a one-page list of "guidelines" for this exercise.
It's going to be a long afternoon.

After an outdoor work period, you take a nice hot shower. As you change into
some fresh clothes, you get a whiff of an intriguing aroma from the kitchen. It turns
out to be a delicious curry made by Sabine, who traveled all the way from Germany to
assist at this retreat. She delivers your tray to you and you thank her for the meal.

By the time the bedtime bell rings you are tired, even though your body has been
sedentary much of the day. Yet you are learning some very important things about
yourself that have the potential to change your life in a profound way. You trust the
process and continue making this investment in your future by studying the text of your
life. What's next?

198

DAY FIVE

Today you continue with your reflection on the theme of *Lying and Stealing*. Much of the time in a Naikan Retreat is spent reflecting on individuals, but the themes of lying and stealing relate to anyone and everyone in your past. What are some of the ways we lie over the course of our lives?

Blatant Lies

"I told my boss that I was late because of a flat tire but actually I overslept." This is a blatant lie. When we make something up to deliberately create a false impression, most of us would agree that we're lying. How often do you create such a lie? Check it out for yourself. Be on the lookout for the impulse to lie and count how many times you give in to it over the course of a week or a month.

Lies of Omission

There are lies of omission, for example, when we're lying through our silence rather than through our words. If we are selling a car, and neglect to mention that it sometimes stalls in the rain, that silence is misleading. It is creating a false impression. It creates a distorted picture of reality for self-serving purposes.

Lies of Action or Inaction

If we break commitments, vows, or promises, we are lying through our actions. If we say one thing and then do another, those actions or inactions are, in effect, lies. They prevent us from being true to our words and cause others to lose confidence and trust in us.

There are also different ways we steal. There's the obvious stealing of material objects. But there's also the stealing of time or peace of mind, stealing privacy by eavesdropping or snooping, etc.

Reflecting on lying and stealing allows us to recognize our history of dishonesty. When we recall those situations in which we chose to deceive or mislead, we can see very clearly how our greed, insecurity and selfishness operated in our life and how our conduct negatively and unfairly impacted on others.

These reflections bring awareness of our harshness and condemnation of others. A hard-hearted position is difficult to sustain if we are genuinely in touch with our own failures. When we see our own shortcomings and weaknesses, we are less likely to be self-righteous, arrogant, and judgmental. It is when we are blind to our own transgressions that we are quick to judge and slow to forgive.

Keep a log of your lying and stealing for a set period of time. Hold your discoveries in the forefront of your mind and notice if they have any impact on your relationships.

DAY SIX AND SEVEN

You've been here for five full days and you've done over 70 hours of self-reflection. You've witnessed your life, not as a smooth full-length film, but in bits and pieces of video – a mosaic of how you've lived and conducted yourself in relation to others. This final stretch is perhaps the most important part of the retreat. Even though you're tired, you are now deeply immersed in the process. You have a greater capacity to reflect on your life during this time than ever before.

You have some choices of who to reflect on, but you'll also be getting assigned exercises to close out the final 24 hours.

One of those exercises is to select a difficult period in your life and to examine that period through the lens of Naikan reflection. It could be a time you were seriously ill, a relationship breakup, or even something more traumatic.

There's also an exercise that asks you to do Naikan reflection on an accomplishment. Another asks you to reflect on your relationship to the environment. What have I received from the environment? What have I given? And what troubles and difficulties have I caused the environment? If we all reflected on these questions regularly, what difference might there be in our society's relationship to the planet?

In the bathroom, you notice a quote on the dresser next to the clean towels. It's from Dzigar Kongtrul, a Tibetan Buddhist teacher who is considered to be Pema Chodron's personal teacher. The quote says:

200

"We are imprisoned in this pain by a sense of self-importance. Self-importance is an underlying clinging we have to 'I, I, I, Me, Me, Me, Mine, Mine, Mine.' This colors all of our experience. It takes courage to go beyond self-importance to see who we really are – but this is our path."

Five days ago you might have simply read the quote like a mild breeze passing though the leaves of an aspen. But today, with your heightened awareness and sensitivity, it touches you deeply. It does take courage to go beyond self-importance. You've already started down that path.

When the retreat ends, you go outside for a walk. The apple blossoms are in full bloom. The sun is beaming down on you. The unmowed grass in the yard is smiling at you. The birds are singing in three-part harmony. You hear a bell. Time for the final meal – time to share a meal with everyone who has been present here for the past week, each on their own unique journey.

You sit down to a stack of homemade mango-walnut pancakes, fruit, tofu, coffee and more. You have a chance to speak now. You are invited to say something about the week. What will you say? How do you express your experience in words? Have your reflections been the tools you have used to cultivate a garden with your mind and heart? Or, are you, yourself, the garden? And who has been doing the gardening the past week?

My Life is Not What I Thought

by Ron Hogen Green

I thought my life was mine!
How could I get what I want?
How could I not get what I don't want?
How to control and manipulate,
subtly
perhaps unconsciously,
the people and circumstances around me.

I thought life was designed as a game of giving me what I want.
Having been fulfilled by a wanted thing,
better be on the lookout for the next shiny object.

Anything can be used to feed my endless wanting
in the name of my fulfillment.
marriage,
love,
spiritual practice.

I am seeing my life as the outside of a hollow ball that has no true center.
I am holding on to it as hard as I can.
I want to truly love.
I want to truly be loved.
How can I?
I only see what I want.

My life is busy, full of self-involvement.
I do not see,
I do not hear,
I only want.

I'm tired of the energy of grasping.
The fear of not getting.
The anxiety of not having.
The sorrow of disconnection.

Where is the life I long for?
What is the reality that is larger than my self-centered frame?

I want to know I am forgiven.
I want to know I can forgive.
I want to love and receive whatever you offer.

Do I want to see more of my life than the wanting?
What happened? What truly happened?
Do I really want to know?
I do.

I'm tired of thinking I know something about what happened.
I want to know more than my stories and fairy tales.

If I can see more I can love
and be loved,
no matter what I see.
Where to begin?

Not with answers –
with questions.

The question of what my mother gave to me.
Nothing. Or not much. Or only pain.

Looking back with a child's eyes
And a grown up mind
I find clothing. She washed all my clothing.
Even the pajamas I peed in.

She made me meals. Hundreds of them.
No thousands of them.
I remember some of them.
She shopped for food.
She worked.
It doesn't stop.
It's all there – all of it.
I've stepped into a time machine.
Only the time ran out.
For now.

What did I give her?
What did I give my mom?
A potholder.
A postcard from camp.
What I gave her was for me.
It had nothing to do with giving.

What troubles did I cause her?
Well, as the song goes,
every move I made,
every step I took:
Visits to the principal's office,
fights at school,
stealing candy,
and money.

The lies I told,
the cursing to her face,
now seen in exquisite specificity.

I remember how I felt when it happened,
but now I feel her.
Her.
For the first time – OH!

My life was never what I thought.
Yes, there was pain, struggle, difficulty.
But while I was concentrating on getting mine,
the entire time,
I was succored,
held in loving arms,
even if it didn't feel that way at the time.

I want to truly love.
I want to truly be loved.
I have been loved.
I just couldn't see
beyond what I wanted.

"There is an ancient Chinese art of painting on porcelain. It requires, more than skill and precision, a deep trust and patience in the process. It involves painting thin layers of pigment, one at a time, on the porcelain, letting each dry and soak into the porcelain itself. But even when dry, the pigment doesn't yet reveal its color. You never know what the color will be until the porcelain is fired in the kiln − that is, until the pigment is burned into the porcelain itself.
This is remarkably like the life of questions that come from living. We use the brush of our feelings to paint our questions into our heart. But only after the fire of experience, only after our felt questions are burned by experience into our heart, only then do we see the color of truth emerge."

Mark Nepo

Acknowledgements

I offer this collection of essays as a tribute to the power of self-reflection and its potential to change our minds and soften our hearts. I am honored to be the curator of this word museum and, as with any museum, the value of the collection is based on the individual works of art. In this collection you hear a variety of voices, each with its own style, testifying to our capacity to examine ourselves honestly and sincerely. My thanks to each of the contributors for making this book possible.

I offer my deepest thanks to my assistant editor, Morris Sullivan, who helped get this project off the ground and to Ben Pease, the ToDo Institute's coordinator of educational resources, who provided the energy and time to help move the book through its final stages of birth.

Gerald Sprankel did an exquisite job of designing the interior of the book and Amanda Coyle contributed her artistic eye to design a lovely cover that conveys something authentic and subtle about the spirit of the book.

Special thanks to Judith Harris, who offered the precision of her copyediting and proofreading, and to Terry J. Benzie and Heather Pendley who helped us do the final proofreading prior to publication.

The roots of this book are grounded in a process of self-reflection known as Naikan which was developed by Yoshimoto Ishin and initially introduced to the U.S.

by David Reynolds. I was fortunate to have wonderful teachers who helped me delve into my own personal self-examination. They include Mrs. Kinuko Yoshimoto, Rev. Shue Usami, Rev. Kenryu T. Tsuji, Professor Akira Ishii, and Nagashima Masahiro. I have also had the good fortune to engage in dialogue with my contemporary colleagues who have been involved with Naikan for decades. They include Ron "Hogen" Green, Sue Cole, Trudy Boyle and Sabine Kaspari (Germany).

Whenever I introduce Naikan in a presentation I use my wife Linda as an example. Her support takes many different forms. In this book she is a contributor, and has also helped with editing and proofreading. She has been my partner in running Naikan retreats at the ToDo Institute for the past 28 years. Most importantly, she has been a source of inspiration for me to continue to write, teach and develop innovative approaches to offering self-reflection to others. Virtually everything I write has been influenced by her own views and ideas. Thank you, Linda, for being my teacher, colleague, and wife.

Whether you have a printed copy of this book or a digital one, there is a hidden network that makes it possible for this book to get from me to you. It's a network that includes trees, paper mills, digital printing presses, trucks, delivery people, software, hardware, the Internet . . . the network goes deeper than we realize. The process of growing a book from a seed in an author's mind to a blossoming idea in the reader's mind is unfathomable and it teaches us the depth of interdependence on which our lives are supported.

To recognize this interdependence is to become conscious of the basic structure of the universe at work.

Contributors

Gregg Krech, Editor

Gregg Krech is an author, editor, and one of the leading authorities on Japanese Psychology in North America. His work has been featured on public radio and in *THE SUN Magazine, Tricycle, SELF, Utne Reader, Counseling Today, Cosmopolitan and Experience Life*.

His book, *Naikan: Gratitude, Grace, and the Japanese Art of Self-Reflection*, won a Spirituality and Health Magazine Award for Best Books of 2002 and has been translated into five languages. His book, *The Art of Taking Action: Lessons from Japanese Psychology*, is an Amazon best seller. His newest book, *Tunneling for Sunlight: 18 Maxims for Meeting Life's Challenges*, will be released in December, 2017.

Krech and his wife Linda are the founders of **The ToDo Institute**, a non-profit center in Vermont that uses Japanese Psychology as an alternative to traditional Western approaches to psychology. Over the past 25 years, Krech has introduced Japanese Psychology, particularly Naikan Therapy, Morita Therapy and Kaizen, to thousands of people through his workshops, speaking engagements and online courses.

His work is a blend of the psychological, the spiritual and the practical based on values such as purpose, gratitude, mindfulness, compassion and constructive action. He is a member of the *North American Naikan Council* and Editor of the quarterly journal *Thirty Thousand Days: A Journal for Purposeful Living*.

www.thirtythousanddays.org
www.todoinstitute.org

Morris Sekiyo Sullivan, Assistant Editor

Sensei Morris Sekiyo Sullivan is a Buddhist minister and dharma holder in Rinzai Zen. He is a chaplain at Stetson University; the spiritual head of Volusia Buddhist Fellowship in DeLand, Florida; performs services for English speakers at White Sands Buddhist Center, a Vietnamese monastery in Mims; and meets weekly with Buddhist inmates at Tomoka Correctional Institution. He also speaks regularly to Unitarian Universalist congregations in Central Florida. He was first ordained as a monk in a Thai order before becoming a Sensei with Bright Dawn Center for Oneness Buddhism in 2010. He lives in DeLand with his wife, two dogs, a cat and a ferret.

Kathy Abromeit is a music librarian at the Oberlin Conservatory of Music in Oberlin, OH, and she teaches shamanism in Oberlin's Experimental College.

Blaze Ardman (aka Perri) has been teaching and practicing Morita and Naikan therapies since 1987. An ordained interfaith minister, she has offered Naikan instruction as a volunteer with the Rondout Valley Holistic Health Community, presented workshops at various venues in New York's Hudson Valley, and with Barbara Sarah, co-presented classes in Japanese psychology at Bard College's Lifetime Learning Institute.

Linda Anderson Krech, LICSW, is the Program Director of the ToDo Institute and a regular contributor to the journal, Thirty Thousand Days. Linda has a special interest in the application of Japanese Psychology to parenting, relationships and psychiatric issues, and is in the process of developing a program entitled Solving the Food Koan. She is the author of Little Dreams Come True: A Practical Guide to Spiritual Parenting (2006).

Kurt Barstow is a massage therapist, art historian, and freelance writer from the Los Angeles area. He is a volunteer with The Heart Touch Project, offering compassionate touch for people at the end stages of life.

Andy Bienkowski is a retired mental health professional and is the author of Radical Gratitude and Other Life Lessons Learned in Siberia and One Life to Give: A Path to Finding Yourself by Helping Others.

Clark Chilson is an associate professor at the University of Pittsburgh, where he teaches on religion in Asia and Buddhist psychology. He is the author of Secrecy's Power: Covert Shin Buddhists in Japan and Contradictions of Concealment (2014). He has done four intensive Naikan retreats in Tokyo. As a member of the Naikan North American Council, he contributes blog posts to its website. An article he wrote in Japanese on Naikan and Buddhism appeared in the July 2017 issue of the Japanese Journal of Clinical Psychology.

Margarita Delgado Creamer, Ph.D. currently teaches Asian religions at the University of Pittsburgh. She specializes in Chinese Buddhism and is particularly interested in contemplative practices, the role of religious material culture in intercultural exchange and environmental ethics. She has studied and worked in Asia, Europe, North and South America but her favorite place to inhabit is the space created by the Naikan retreat.

Melissa Ericksen Cocuzza has been studying Japanese psychology for over 20 years. She lives in Southington, Connecticut and is the founder of A Balanced Life, a company which coordinates Health & Wellness Expos. She is also a Justice of the Peace and has performed over 150 weddings.

Michele Faris is a licensed psychologist in Colorado who has lived and worked in Fort Collins for over 40 years. She works as a senior staff psychologist at Colorado State University's counseling center and maintains a small private practice. She lives with her partner Rick with whom she shares four beautiful daughters.

Romola Georgia lives in Palo, Alto, CA where she is a Master Gardener specializing in edible and sustainable landscaping. She plays the cello and has completed her Certification in Japanese Psychology through the ToDo Institute.

Ron Hogen Green Sensei has been engaged in formal Zen practice since 1978, and was in residential training at the Zen Mountain Monastery for twelve years as a lay person and monastic. He received Dharma Transmission from Geoffrey Shugen Arnold Sensei, at Zen Mountain Monastery in 2016. Hogen divides his time between teaching Zen at the Zen Center of New York and his home in Danville, Pennsylvania.

Kara Jacobs retired as a child welfare worker in 2015 and has since completed a Hospice internship and become a licensed clinical social worker, opening her own practice.

Kiki Latimer teaches courses at the Osher Lifelong Learning Institute at the University of Rhode Island to help students understand our interconnectedness and the importance of gratitude in our lives. She is a children's author, speaker, and presentations coach and lives in Hope Valley, Rhode Island.

Otavio Lilla lives in São Paulo, Brazil, where he is a writer and co-owner of Mistral Wines.

Les MacFarlane is a teacher and curriculum leader with the Ottawa Catholic School Board. He is the author of Teaching Language with the Saints (2015, Novalis) and has been professor in the faculty of education at the University of Ottawa. Les is certified in Constructive Living and has assisted at multiple programs focused on Japanese Psychology at the ToDo Institute.

Margaret McKenzie is a social worker and Zen teacher currently living in Glen Ellyn, Illinois. She currently works in the inpatient psychiatric unit of a community hospital and leads a meditation group for students and staff at the local community college.

Viveca Monahan is credentialed as a professional certified coach (PCC) through the International Coach Federation (ICF), and as a certified mentor coach through Invite CHANGE. She is also an ADD coach with training obtained through the ADD Coach Academy and has received her certificate in Japanese Psychology from the ToDo Institute where she has assisted in conducting Naikan retreats.. She lives and works with playful irreverence in Seattle.

Denise Mosher is a campus minister at Western Oregon University and Oblate at St. John's (Benedictine) Abbey in Collegeville, MN. She holds a certificate in Japanese Psychology from ToDo Institute. She and husband Paul have been a couple for twenty years—"over half my life."

Alexandra Newton Rios, bilingual poet, translator and professor, was raised in Manhattan and lived in the small city of San Miguel de Tucumán, one of the poorest regions of northwestern Argentina, for twenty-three years. She is a graduate of the University of Iowa with an MFA in English from the Writers' Workshop and an MFA in Translation in Comparative Literature. She is the author of three bilingual editions of poetry published by Ediciones Magna in Argentina. She turned to nonfiction to write about life in a third world country with The Light of Argentina: A Philosophy Diary Conversations with Hannah Arendt, published in 2014.

Christina Newton, lives in Sea Cliff, NY and wears many hats: mother, wife, daughter, sister, friend, yoga student, yoga teacher, computer tutor, bookkeeper, landlord, homeowner, poet, writer, and artist. She is a lover of the ocean & mountains, of being outside, of traveling, and above all she is a lifelong learner, trying to find balance while practicing gratitude and connecting to the joy of being alive.

Carol O'Dowd, MPA, M.Div., MI found her prior 20 years working for and with governments as manager/consultant combined with 13 years as an ordained Buddhist priest useful for getting her son out of Kerobokan Prison, Indonesia in 2015. She used her certifications in Japanese Psychology, Applied Existential Psychology and Mindfulness to support her counseling services there and as a Registered Psychotherapist in Colorado. The book she is   writing shares how to escape from prisons, including the ones we create for ourselves.

Anne-Carine Oskarsen is currently residing in Belgium where she works in an organic food store. She has studied macrobiotics for almost 10 years, and is a trained shiatsu therapist.

Jane Palmer is a fiction writer, communications consultant and community organizer in Reading, Pennsylvania. She works with Keystone Progress, a communications and collaborative organizing hub for the progressive community in Pennsylvania. "Mind the Gap" was originally delivered as a sermon at the First Unitarian Universalist Church of Berks County, where Jane has been an active member for almost 20 years. She lives in a little stone house with a red door with her husband, Bill Bellows, and two dogs.

Rabbi Rami Shapiro is an award–winning author of over thirty books on religion and spirituality. Rami received rabbinical ordination from the Hebrew Union College–Jewish Institute of Religion in 1981, a Ph.D. in religious studies from Union Graduate School in 1985, and initiation into the Ramakrishna Order of Vedanta Hinduism by Swami Swahananda in 2011. A congregational rabbi for 20 years and a Professor of Religious Studies for 10, Rami currently directs the One River Foundation for the Study of Perennial Wisdom. Among Rami's many books are The Sacred Art of Loving–kindness, The Divine Feminine in Biblical Wisdom Literature, and Perennial Wisdom for the Spiritually Independent.

Victoria Register-Freeman is a ToDo Institute member, writer and former B&B owner in Jacksonville, Florida. After teaching for 38 years, she retired to run a bed and breakfast for a decade. She now spends her time visiting grandchildren, learning to play the mountain dulcimer, bicycling and giving Master Gardener presentations. She is a Soul Collage facilitator and the author of Love Stories from the Bible.

Robert Strayhan, M.D. is a psychiatrist in Texarkana, Texas and is affiliated with Christus St. Michael Health System-Texarkana. He received his medical degree from Meharry Medical College and has been in practice for more than 30 years.

Barbara Sarah, LCSW, is an oncology social worker who founded the Oncology Support Program at Benedictine Hospital in Kingston, New York in 1994. She has been practicing and teaching Morita and Naikan therapies since 1988 and is the Director of Third Opinion, a cancer survivor consultation service.

Yoshinori Sato is a clinical psychologist living in San Diego. He works for the California Department of Corrections and Rehabilitation, primarily with mentally ill offenders in the prison system. His main interest is the use of mindfulness in the treatment of depression and anxiety disorders.

Robert Strayhan, M.D., is a psychiatrist in Texarkana, Texas and is affiliated with Christus St. Michael Health System-Texarkana. He received his medical degree from Meharry Medical College and has been in practice for more than 30 years.

Amy Szarkowski, Ph.D., is a member of the faculty of Comparative Cultures at Miyazaki International College in Japan and teaches courses in psychology and counseling. Teaching, traveling, watching the sunrise, learning, playing volley ball, reading, helping others, running, and baking are a few of her passions.

Zoe Weil is the co-founder and president of the Institute for Humane Education (IHE) and is the author of seven books including The World Becomes What We Teach: Educating a Generation of Solutionaries (2016), Most Good, Least Harm: A Simple Principle for a Better World and Meaningful Life (2009), and Above All, Be Kind: Raising a Humane Child in Challenging Times (2003). She received a Master's in Theological Studies from Harvard Divinity School (1988) and a Master's and Bachelor's in English Literature from the University of Pennsylvania (1983).

Gregory Willms (1949-1994) was a psychotherapist having received his MFCC from the University of San Francisco in 1982. He was certified as a Constructive Living Instructor in 1989 and assisted in conducting a Naikan retreat before his untimely death from complications from AIDS in 1994. He was the author of Images for Living: Reflections on the Ox Herding Pictures.

Appendix

Examining the Impact of Naikan Reflection for 30 Days: Results from the ToDo Institute's 2013 Online Course
Gregg Krech

For more than twenty years, I've been teaching a distance learning course in which participants engage in a month of self-reflection based on the Japanese method of self-reflection called Naikan. The course includes readings, video, a discussion forum and my book, Naikan: Gratitude, Grace and the Japanese *Art of Self-Reflection*. The foundation of the course, however, is a series of daily exercises which provide an opportunity for participants to engage in some type of self-reflection continuously for one month.

In November 2013, we had approximately 100 people in the course from seven different countries. At the end of the program, we surveyed participants through a simple online questionnaire to get a sense of how the course affected them. Forty of the participants kindly responded to our survey.

Historically, only a small percentage of participants complete every exercise.

Of those who responded, 45% completed at least 21 exercises, and another 30% completed between 10 and 20 exercises. So overall, the vast majority of respondents completed at least one-third to one-half of the daily exercises.

Discussion

I'd like to discuss two of the key survey questions:

First, *"How would you compare your level of gratitude now with where you were prior to taking this course?"*

The largest group (44%) indicated that they were "slightly more grateful and appreciative now" than before the course started. One person (3%) indicated that there was "no change." The second largest group (38%) indicated they were "significantly more grateful and appreciative now" than before the course started. Finally, and of particular interest, 15% of the respondents agreed with this statement:

I feel there has been a real transformation in me – a dramatic change where I'm truly more appreciative and grateful for my life and for what others have done for me.

So more than half (53%) said the change in their experience of gratitude was significant or transformational. This is really quite extraordinary—particularly the 15% that experienced the change as "transformational." This doesn't mean such a transformation is permanent. But I believe it suggests that, rather than simply a change in one's perspective, there was a "shift" in one's way of understanding life.

This is how I would characterize my own personal experience from doing Naikan reflection in Japan in the late 1980s and early 1990s. I still complain and feel like life is unfair on a regular basis . But underlying those experiences is a foundation of awareness of what has been given to me and how I have been cared for and loved. In other words, my complaints rest on a much larger foundation of gratitude and awareness of what I have been given.

The second question I want to discuss is, *"How would you describe any change in your attitude or outlook during the past month?"*

The three answers that generated the most responses by participants were:

1. I'm more aware of how I'm supported and cared for.
2. I feel more grateful and appreciative of others.
3. I'm more conscious of my own self-centeredness.

The first two responses are not that surprising. They seem in line with the responses to the first question. But let's consider the third response, in which people are more aware of their own self-centeredness. To some, this would seem like a "bad" result. It's certainly not something to which most people would aspire. I think it reveals that sincere self-reflection is (and should be) more than simply an effort to feel more grateful.

Naikan is a method for conducting a thorough self-examination of one's life in relation to others. To the extent we succeed at this, we may come face to face with incidents and events we are ashamed of – those in which we acted out of self-interest and which resulted in the suffering of others. From a mental health perspective, awareness of one's own self-centeredness is not popular. But from a spiritual standpoint, such awareness leads to humility and can open one to a deeper sense of faith. Empirical research on humility shows that it's a characteristic with greater value than we might expect:

> *Humility has been linked with better academic performance, job performance, and excellence in leadership. Humble people have better social relationships . . . A recent set of studies also shows that humility is a consistent predictor of generosity. People who are humble tend to be more generous with both their time and their money.*
>
> – Psychology Today

221

Gratitude & Grace

The last point I would like to make is the relationship between gratitude and grace. We can be grateful for something, but still have the view that we earned or deserved what we received. For example, if you worked hard last week, you can appreciate your paycheck, but still feel that you earned it through your efforts. In Japanese, we call this jiriki (self-power).

However, when you become aware of your mistakes, faults, weaknesses and self-centered ego, you may be humbled by how you have conducted your life. At least in some arenas, you may feel grateful for things and people, without the sense that you earned or deserved them. This is grace, or, in Japanese tariki (other-power). For example, let's say you were sick last week and didn't work at all. But you still were paid. If you reflect deeply on this, you may feel very fortunate (or you may just think, "Hey, everyone gets sick leave – what's the big deal?). In any case, tariki brings us much closer to an experience of faith or trust in something beyond ourselves.

The survey I have been discussing was not designed as academic research. It is not based on a double-blind control group study. But I do think it gives us a glimpse of the importance of self-reflection in our lives and the connection between such reflection and the experience of gratitude, grace, humility, faith and trust.

Austin, Michale W., Ph.D. "Humility." Psychology Today. N.p., 27 June 2012. Web. 27 Apr. 2016.

References

Chilson, Clark. *Secrecy's Power: Covert Shin Buddhists in Japan and Contradictions of Conceal-ment*. Honolulu: University of Hawaii Press, 2014.

Dostoyevsky, Fyodor. "'The Peasant Marey," in *A Writer's Diary* (Northwestern University Press, 1994).

Emmons, Robert. Thanks: *How the New Science of Gratitude Can Make You Happier*. Boston: Houghton Mifflin, 2007.

Haguri, Gyodo. *The Awareness of Self*. Anaheim, CA: Buddhist Education Center, 1967, 2015.

Haneda, Nobuo. *Dharma Breeze: Essays on Shin Buddhism*. Berkeley: Maida Center on Buddhism, 2007.

Ishii, Akira and Hartl, Josef. *Das Wesen von Naikan (The Essence of Naikan)*. Vienna: Altes Wissen, Neue Wege, 2000.

Kongtrul, Dzigar. It's Up to You: *The Practice of Self-Reflection on the Buddhist Path*. Boston: Shambhala, 2006.

Krech, Gregg. *Naikan: Gratitude, Grace and the Japanese Art of Self-Reflection*. Berkeley: Stone Bridge Press, 2002.

Krech, Gregg. *A Natural Approach to Mental Wellness: Japanese Psychology and the Skills We Need for Psychological and Spiritual Health*. Monkton, VT: ToDo Institute Books, 2000, 2015.

Krech, Gregg. Naikan: *The Practice of Attention and Reflection*. Middlebury, VT: ToDo Institute Books, 1995.

Leddy, Mary Jo. *Radical Gratitude*. Maryknoll, NY: Orbis Books, 2002.

Nishida, Norimasa. *Naikan: Self-reflection for Happiness and Success*. Hakone Nat'l Park Naikan Training Center, 2001.

Ozawa-de Silva, Chikako. *Psychotherapy and Religion in Japan: The Japanese Introspection practice of Naikan*. New York: Routledge Press, 2006.

Reynolds, David. *The Quiet Therapies: Japanese Pathways to Personal Growth*. Honolulu: University of Hawaii Press, 1980.

Steindl-Rast, David. *Gratefulness, the Heart of Prayer*. New York: Paulist Press, 1984.

Unno, Taitetsu. *Gratitude: It's Source and Power*. San Francisco: Buddhist Churches of America, 1991.

Winter, Angela. *Many Thanks: Gregg Krech on The Revolutionary Practice Of Gratitude*. The Sun Magazine, 2004.

81958722R00132

Made in the USA
Lexington, KY
24 February 2018